WC
FACTS

Collins Gem: World Cup Facts was not prepared, authorized, licensed or endorsed by any person, entity or organization involved in the sponsorship of the England football team, the 1998 World Cup, FIFA and/or ISL.

First published in 1998 by
CollinsWillow
an imprint of HarperCollins *Publishers*
London

© HarperCollins*Publishers* 1998

1 3 5 7 9 8 6 4 2

All rights reserved. No part of this publication may be
reproduced, stored in a retrieval system, or transmitted, in
any form or by any means, electronic, mechanical, photo-
copying, recording or otherwise, without the prior written
permission of the publishers.

Parts of this book are published in *The Complete Book of the
World Cup*

A CIP catalogue record for this book is available from the
British Library.

ISBN 0 00 218854 6

Created and produced by Flame Tree Publishing,
a part of The Foundry Creative Media Company Ltd,
The Long House, Antrobus Road,
Chiswick, London W4 5HY.
Grateful thanks to Helen Courtney, Dave Jones
and Sonya Newland.

Printed and bound in Italy by Amadeus S.p.A.

COLLINS GEM

WORLD CUP
FACTS

Text by Cris Freddi

Collins
Willow

CONTENTS

NEW
WORLD ORDER

Uruguay 1930

FIVE COUNTRIES applied to stage the first World
Cup tournament, only for four to step quickly aside
once all the credentials were on the table. Uruguay were
clearly the big players. In some reports it comes across as a
surprising decision, as if the game's showpiece had been
offered to a Third World shanty town, but in fact
Montevideo was a thriving city and port. 1930 was the
centenary of Uruguayan independence and the country's
exchequer was buoyant enough to build a grand new stadium and to guarantee the expenses of every country that
took part. This seems to have cut little ice with most of
Europe, however. Regular jet travel was still in the future,
so the financial guarantees persuaded only four countries
to make the ocean voyage. The real contenders stayed at
home: Hungary, Austria, Italy, Germany, Spain – while
England and Scotland, as strong as anyone, weren't even
eligible, having resigned from FIFA over the question of
'broken time' payments in 1928.

All of which didn't really matter very much. Even
against Europe's finest, Uruguay would have been expected
to win. In 1924 they'd played outside South America for
the first time, winning the Olympic title in Paris. After thrashing
Yugoslavia 7-0 and the hosts 5-1, they outplayed the Swiss
3-0 in the final, their stern defence buttressing some dazzling
inter-passing up front. Four years later they won it again.

It wasn't just that they happened to have a strong pool of players. What really separated the leading South American countries from European opposition was a familiarity with tournaments arranged along World Cup lines; several matches played in the space of a month or so. Ideas on physical preparation and training camps were in advance of anything in most of Europe at the time. The only real opposition was likely to come from Argentina, who'd taken them to a replay in the Olympic final two years earlier and beaten them 2-0 to win the Copa América in between. The four European entries weren't particularly good, but at least they were there, and one or two were about to play more than just a bit-part in history.

The formalities before the first Final: the captains Nasazzi (left) and Ferreira with referee Langenus.

Groups

GROUP 1

	P	W	D	L	F	A	PTS
Argentina	3	3	0	0	10	4	6
Chile	3	2	0	1	5	3	4
France	3	1	0	2	4	3	2
Mexico	3	0	0	3	4	13	0

Argentina qualified for the semi-finals.

GROUP 2

	P	W	D	L	F	A	PTS
Yugoslavia	2	2	0	0	6	1	4
Brazil	2	1	0	1	5	2	2
Bolivia	2	0	0	2	0	8	0

Yugoslavia qualified for the semi-finals.

GROUP 3

	P	W	D	L	F	A	PTS
Uruguay	2	2	0	0	5	0	4
Romania	2	1	0	1	3	5	2
Peru	2	0	0	2	1	4	0

Uruguay qualified for the semi-finals.

GROUP 4

	P	W	D	L	F	A	PTS
USA	2	2	0	0	6	0	4
Paraguay	2	1	0	1	1	3	2
Belgium	2	0	0	2	0	4	0

USA qualified for the semi-finals.

Semi-finals

26 July 1930 • Centenário, Montevideo • 72,886 •
John Langenus (BEL)

ARGENTINA (1) 6 Monti 20, Scopelli 56, Stábile
69, 87, Peucelle 80, 85
USA (0) 1 Brown 89

ARGENTINA *Botasso, Della Torre, Paternóster, J. Evaristo, Monti,
Orlandini, Peucelle, Scopelli, Stábile, Ferreira (c), M. Evaristo.*
USA *Douglas, Wood, Moorhouse, Gallagher, Tracy, Gonsalves,
Auld, Brown, Patenaude, Florie (c), McGhee.*

27 July 1930 • Centenário, Montevideo • 79,867 •
Gilberto de Almeida Rego (BRZ)

URUGUAY (3) 6 Cea 18, 67, 72, Anselmo 20, 31,
Iriarte 61
YUGOSLAVIA (1) 1 Vujadinovic 4

URUGUAY *Ballestrero, Nasazzi
(c), Mascheroni, Andrade,
Fernández, Gestido, Dorado,
Scarone, Anselmo, Cea, Iriarte.*
YUGOSLAVIA *Jaksic, Ivkovic (c),
Mihajlovic, Arsenijevic, Stevanovic,
Dokic, Tirnanic, Marjanovic, Bek,
Vujadinovic, Sekulic.*

The first goal in a World Cup Final.

Final

30 July 1930 • Centenário, Montevideo • 68,346 •
John Langenus (BEL)

URUGUAY (1) 4 Dorado 12, Cea 57, Iriarte 68,
Castro 89
ARGENTINA (2) 2 Peucelle 20, Stábile 37

URUGUAY *Ballestrero, Nasazzi (c), Mascheroni, Andrade,
Fernández, Gestido, Dorado, Scarone, Castro, Cea, Iriarte.*
ARGENTINA *Botasso, Della Torre, Paternóster, J. Evaristo, Monti,
Suárez, Peucelle, Varallo, Stábile, Ferreira (c), M. Evaristo.*

LEADING GOALSCORERS 1930

8	Guillermo Stábile	ARG
5	Pedro Cea	URU
4	Bert Patenaude	USA

Uruguay 1930, the first World Cup winners.

THE FULL MONTI

Italy 1934

HAVING STAGED the first World Cup in the right place, FIFA now did the opposite: they handed the second tournament to Italy. Even they must have had reservations, though; it took them eight meetings to make up their minds. Once again the hosts were expected to win, especially as Italy's coach was one of the great early man-managers and strategists. There had been some friction between his centre-half and centre-forward following a league match – so Pozzo made them share a room. He needed this kind of no-prisoners centre-half for his system of play, plus a pair of good wingers – and he knew where to find them, helping himself to a number of South American internationals, on the basis that if they could die for Italy (they were eligible for national service) they could play for Italy.

So in came Filó, capped by Brazil in 1925, and several high-class Argentinians: Demaría who'd played in the 1930 World Cup; Orsi who'd played in the last Olympic final; Guaita on the other wing; and Monti himself, a linchpin at Juventus (four league titles). They were all apparently ineligible, but FIFA turned a blind eye. Among the opposition, Hungary were improving, using the smooth Sárosi at centre-half as well as centre-forward. Czechoslovakia had Plánicka in goal, Nejedly and the forceful Puc up front. Spain had a great goalkeeper in Zamora.

Above all, Austria – managed by the passionate Jewish banker Hugo Meisl – had dominated the early 1930s ('das Wunderteam'), beating Scotland 5-0, Germany 6-0 and 5-0, Switzerland 8-1. Playing the same old Scottish close-passing game as the other Danubians, they arrived in Italy without their fine goalkeeper Rudi Hiden, but still had their share of world-class players: Smistik the attacking centre-half; the prolific Schall; two genuinely great forwards in Bican and the slender Sindelar. They were probably just past their peak (Meisl himself thought so) but had recently beaten Italy 4-2 in Turin. Uruguay, however, stayed away, perhaps in revenge for being snubbed by the main European powers in 1930, or because their team needed rebuilding. Of the other absent friends, England lost in Hungary and Czechoslovakia just before the competition, and Meisl believed they wouldn't have reached the semi-finals.

The tournament had grown too big to be held in a single city, and there were enough entries to warrant a qualifying competition, in which even Italy had to take part. The problems of a knockout system began to show. Mexico had travelled 4,000 miles to play a single match and not even in the competition proper!

The referee and linesmen give the Fascist salute before the Final.

Round 1

27 May 1934 • Nazionale del PNF, Rome •
25,000 • René Mercet (SWI)
ITALY (3) 7 Schiavio 18, 29, 64, Orsi 20,
69,Ferrari 63, Meazza 90
USA (0) 1 Donelli 57

27 May 1934 • Littorio, Trieste • 8,000 •
John Langenus (BEL)
CZECHOSLOVAKIA (0) 2 Puc 48, Nejedly 65
ROMANIA (1) 1 Dobay 11

27 May 1934 • Giovanni Berta, Florence • 8,000 •
Francesco Mattea (ITA)
GERMANY (1) 5 Kobierski 28, Siffling 47, Conen
67, 70, 86
BELGIUM (2) 2 Voorhoof 32, 44

27 May 1934 • Benito Mussolini, Turin • 15,000 •
Joop van Moorsel (HOL)
AUSTRIA (1) 3 Sindelar 44, Schall 93, Bican 109
FRANCE (1) 2 Nicolas 18, Verriest pen 115

27 May 1934 • Luigi Ferraris, Genoa • 30,000 •
Alfred Birlem (GER)
SPAIN (3) 3 Iraragorri pen 17, Lángara 23, 28
BRAZIL (0) 1 Leônidas 5

27 May 1934 • San Siro, Milan • 35,000 •
Ivan Eklind (SWE)
SWITZERLAND (2) 3 Kielholz 6, 43, Abegglen 66
HOLLAND (1) 2 Smit 29, Vente 69

27 May 1934 • Littoriale, Bologna • 19,000 •
Eugen Braun (AUT)
SWEDEN (1) 3 Jonasson 9, 67, Kroon 80
ARGENTINA (1) 2 Belis 3, Galateo 50

27 May 1934 • Giorgio Ascarelli, Naples •
8,000 • Rinaldo Barlassina (ITA)
HUNGARY (2) 4 Teleki 11, Toldi 31, 61,
Vincze 54
EGYPT (2) 2 Fawzi 39, 43

Quarter-finals

31 May 1934 • San Siro, Milan • 16,000 •
Rinaldo Barlassina (ITA)
GERMANY (0) 2 Hohmann 60, 62
SWEDEN (0) 1 Dunker 82

31 May 1934 • Littoriale,
Bologna • 14,000 • Francesco Mattea (ITA)
AUSTRIA (1) 2 Horvath 5, Zischek 51
HUNGARY (0) 1 Sárosi pen 62

31 May 1934 • Benito Mussolini, Turin • 9,000 •
Alois Beranek (AUT)
CZECHOSLOVAKIA (1) 3 Svoboda 23,
Sobotka 49, Nejedly 83
SWITZERLAND (1) 2 Kielholz 18, Jäggi 80

31 May 1934 • Giovanni Berta, Florence •
40,000 • Louis Baert (BEL)
ITALY (1) (1) 1 Ferrari 45
SPAIN (1) (1) 1 Regueiro 31

1 June 1934 **REPLAY** • Giovanni Berta, Florence •
40,000 • René Mercet (SWI)
ITALY (1) 1 Meazza 12
SPAIN (0) 0

Semi-finals

3 June 1934 • San Siro, Milan • 45,000 •
Ivan Eklind (SWE)

ITALY (1) 1 Guaita 19
AUSTRIA (0) 0

ITALY *Combi (c), Monzeglio, Allemandi, Ferraris, Monti,
Bertolini, Guaita, Meazza, Schiavio, Ferrari, Orsi.*
AUSTRIA *Platzer, Cisar, Sesta, Wagner, Smistik (c), Urbanek,
Zischek, Bican, Sindelar, Schall, Viertl.*

....

3 June 1934 • Nazionale del PNF, Rome •
13,000 • Rinaldo Barlassina (ITA)

CZECHOSLOVAKIA (1) 3 Nejedly 21, 69, 80
GERMANY (0) 1 Noack 59

CZECHOSLOVAKIA *Plánicka (c), Burgr, Ctyroky, Kostálek,*
Cambal, Krcil, Junek, Svoboda, Sobotka, Nejedly, Puc.
GERMANY *Kress, Haringer, Busch, Zielinski, Szepan, Bender,*
Lehner, Siffling, Conen, Noack, Kobierski.

3rd-place Final

7 June 1934 • Giorgio Ascarelli, Naples •
7,000 • Albino Carraro (ITA)

GERMANY (3) 3 Lehner 24 sec, 42, Conen 29
AUSTRIA (1) 2 Horvath 30, Sesta 55

GERMANY *Jakob, Janes, Busch, Zielinski, Münzenberg, Bender,*
Lehner, Siffling, Conen, Szepan (c), Heidemann.
AUSTRIA *Platzer, Cisar, Sesta, Wagner, Smistik, Urbanek,*
Zischek, Braun, Bican, Horvath (c), Viertl.

Opposite: Mean, moody and machiavellian, the first
European team to win the World Cup.

Final

10 June 1934 • Nazionale del PNF, Rome •
50,000 • Ivan Eklind (SWE)

ITALY (0) (1) 2 Orsi 81, Schiavio 95
CZECHOSLOVAKIA (0) (1) 1 Puc 71

ITALY *Combi (c), Monzeglio, Allemandi, Ferraris, Monti, Bertolini, Guaita, Meazza, Schiavio, Ferrari, Orsi.*
CZECHOSLOVAKIA *Plánicka (c), Zenísek, Ctyroky, Kostálek, Cambal, Krcil, Junek, Svoboda, Sobotka, Nejedly, Puc.*

LEADING GOALSCORERS 1934

5	Oldrich Nejedly	CZE
4	Edmund Conen	GER
4	Angelo Schiavio	ITA

THE JUDGMENT OF PARIS

France 1938

THE WORLD CUP was coming back to the land of its fathers, but any celebrations were tempered by events elsewhere. Austria, one of the great football powers, wasn't even a country any more, swallowed up by the *Anschlüss*. Others were soon to follow, including Czechoslovakia, where the Nazis had taken the Sudetenland without a peep from the West. There was civil war in Spain. And Italy, now firmly established as Germany's sidekick, were still strong on the football field.

Only the inside-forwards Meazza and Ferrari remained from the 1934 team. Three others came in from the side that had won the 1936 Olympics, and there was only one South American this time, the Uruguayan Andreolo in Monti's place. Above all, the latest centre-forward, Silvio Piola, was the best in Europe.

Czechoslovakia still had Plánicka, Nejedly and Puc. Brazil, as usual, hadn't played for more than a year. Hungary were full of goals, Sárosi scoring seven, no less, in an 8-3 win over Czechoslovakia, who had Plánicka in goal. The other goal came from the new young striker Zsengellér, who later scored five in the 11-1 qualifying win over Greece. Uruguay again didn't turn up. Nor did Argentina, who'd won the Copa América the previous year (with Guaita back in the team). Meanwhile, a month before the tournament, England had won 6-3 in Germany and 4-2 in France, fielding players like Matthews, Bastin, Drake and Hapgood. Still outside FIFA, they apparently turned down an invitation to take Austria's place.

One of the official posters for the 1938 tournament.

Round 1

4 June 1938 • Parc des Princes, Paris • 27,152 •
John Langenus (BEL)
SWITZERLAND (1) (1) 1 Abegglen 43
GERMANY (1) (1) 1 Gauchel 29

9 June 1938 **REPLAY** • Parc des Princes, Paris •
20,025 • Ivan Eklind (SWE)
SWITZERLAND (1) 4 Walaschek 42, Bickel 64,
Abegglen 75, 78
GERMANY (2) 2 Hahnemann 8, Lörtscher o.g. 22

5 June 1938 • Chapou, Toulouse • 6,707 •
Giuseppe Scarpi (ITA)
CUBA (1) (2) 3 Socorro 44, 103, Magriña 69
ROMANIA (1) (2) 3 Bindea 35, Barátky 88,
Dobay 105

9 June 1938 **REPLAY** • Chapou, Toulouse • 7,536 •
Alfred Birlem (GER)
CUBA (0) 2 Socorro 51, Fernández 57
ROMANIA (1) 1 Dobay 35

5 June 1938 • Vélodrome, Rheims • 9,091 •
Roger Conrié (FRA)
HUNGARY (4) 6 Kohut 14, Toldi 16, Sárosi 25,
88, Zsengellér 30, 67
DUTCH EAST INDIES (0) 0

5 June 1938 • Olympique (Colombes), Paris •
30,454 • Hans Wüthrich (SWI)
FRANCE (2) 3 Veinante 35 sec, Nicolas 11, 69
BELGIUM (1) 1 Isemborghs 19

5 June 1938 • Cavée Verte, Le Havre • 10,550 •
Lucien Leclercq (FRA)
CZECHOSLOVAKIA (0) (0) 3 Kostálek 93, Zeman
111, Nejedly 118
HOLLAND (0) (0) 0

5 June 1938 • De la Meinau, Strasbourg •
13,452 • Ivan Eklind (SWE)
BRAZIL (3) (4) 6 Leônidas 18, 93, 104, Romeu 25,
Perácio 44, 71
POLAND (1) (4) 5 Scherfke pen 23, Wilimowski
53, 59, 89, 118

5 June 1938 • Vélodrome, Marseille •
18,826 • Alois Beranek (GER)
ITALY (1) (1) 2 Ferraris 2, Piola 94
NORWAY (0) (1) 1 Brustad 83

SWEDEN bye (**AUSTRIA** withdrew)

Quarter-finals

12 June 1938 • Fort Carré, Antibes • 6,846 • Gustav Krist (CZE)
SWEDEN (4) 8 H. Andersson 9, 81, 89, Wetterström 22, 37, 44, Keller 80, Nyberg 84
CUBA (0) 0

12 June 1938 • Victor Boucquey, Lille • 14,800 • Rinaldo Barlassina (ITA)
HUNGARY (1) 2 Sárosi 42, Zsengellér 89
SWITZERLAND (0) 0

12 June 1938 • Olympique (Colombes), Paris • 58,455 • Louis Baert (BEL)
ITALY (1) 3 Colaussi 9, Piola 52, 72
FRANCE (1) 1 Heisserer 10

12 June 1938 • Parc Lescure, Bordeaux • 22,021 • Paul von Hertzka (HUN)
BRAZIL (1) (1) 1 Leônidas 30
CZECHOSLOVAKIA (0) (1) 1 Nejedly pen 65

14 June 1938 **REPLAY** • Parc Lescure, Bordeaux • 18,141 • Georges Capdeville (FRA)
BRAZIL (0) 2 Leônidas 57, Roberto 62
CZECHOSLOVAKIA (1) 1 Kopecky 25

Opposite: Goalmouth action from the Final. (l-r):
Olivieri, Locatelli, Sárosi, Foni, Andreolo.

Semi-finals

16 June 1938 • Parc des Princes, Paris •
20,155 • Lucien Leclercq (FRA)

HUNGARY (3) 5 Jacobsson o.g. 19, Titkos 37,
Zsengellér 39, 85, Sárosi 65
SWEDEN (1) 1 Nyberg 35 sec

HUNGARY *Szabó, Korányi, Biró, Szalay, Turay, Lázár, Sas,
Zsengellér, Sárosi (c), Toldi, Titkos.*
SWEDEN *Abrahamsson, Eriksson, Källgren, Almgren, Jacobsson,
Svanström, Wetterström, Keller (c), H. Andersson, Jonasson, Nyberg.*

16 June 1938 • Vélodrome, Marseille •
33,000 • Hans Wüthrich (SWI)

ITALY (0) 2 Colaussi 55, Meazza pen 60
BRAZIL (0) 1 Romeu 87

ITALY *Olivieri, Foni, Rava, Serantoni, Andreolo, Locatelli, Biavati, Meazza (c), Piola, Ferrari, Colaussi.*
BRAZIL *Walter, Domingos, Machado, Zezé Procópio, Martim Silveira (c), Afonsinho, Lopes, Luiz M.Oliveira, Romeu, Perácio, Patesko.*

3rd-place Final

19 June 1938 • Parc Lescure, Bordeaux • 12,500 •
John Langenus (BEL)

BRAZIL (1) 4 Romeu 44, Leônidas 63, 74, Perácio 80
SWEDEN (2) 2 Jonasson 28, Nyberg 38

BRAZIL *Batatais, Domingos, Machado, Zezé Procópio, Brandão, Afonsinho, Roberto, Romeu, Leônidas (c), Perácio, Patesko.*
SWEDEN *Abrahamsson, Eriksson, Nilsson, Almgren, Linderholm, Svanström (c), Nyberg, Persson, H. Andersson, Jonasson, Å. Andersson.*

LEADING GOALSCORERS 1938

7	Leônidas da Silva	BRZ
5	Gyula Zsengellér	HUN
5	György Sárosi	HUN
5	Silvio Piola	ITA

Final

19 June 1938 • Olympique (Colombes), Paris •
45,124 • Georges Capdeville (FRA)

ITALY (3) 4 Colaussi 6, 35, Piola 16, 82
HUNGARY (1) 2 Titkos 7, Sárosi 69

ITALY *Olivieri, Foni, Rava, Serantoni, Andreolo, Locatelli,*
Biavati, Meazza (c), Piola, Ferrari, Colaussi.
HUNGARY *Szabó, Polgár, Biró, Szalay, Szücs, Lázár, Sas,*
Vincze, Sárosi (c), Zsengellér, Titkos.

Italy – the 1938 World Champions.

THE WEIGHT OF SHADOWS

Brazil 1950

THE FIRST TRULY peacetime World Cup in 20 years had its parallels with the previous one: only 13 teams taking part; a league system; a strong host team. This time the idea of four mini-leagues was in place from the start, presumably because FIFA decided knockout matches were an arbitrary way of deciding the best in the world. To emphasize their thinking, the four group winners would qualify for yet another group, the champions to be decided on points.

Several things had happened in 1949 which seemed sure to affect the result of the tournament. Brazil won the Copa América; in Italy, an air crash wiped out the entire Torino squad, the backbone of the national team; Sweden, strong Olympic champions in 1948, lost their best players to Italian clubs.

Uruguay were back in the fold but having a mixed year, and Argentina pulled out yet again. Yugoslavia looked the strongest of the Europeans, Olympic runners-up and packed with world-class players – but the most intriguing entry was from the mother country, taking part for the first time. The 1950 World Cup came a few years too late for England, who'd lost Frank Swift, Tommy Lawton and the incomparable Raich Carter from their team of the immediate post-war years. But Tom Finney was still there, with Billy Wright and Stan Mortensen and (eventually)

Stanley Matthews. At the very least, they were expected to qualify for the final pool.

Brazil had built a new stadium – the biggest in history – with twice the capacity of Wembley. On the first day of the tournament, it still wasn't ready. But the Brazilian public didn't mind too much. Their team seemed to be.

The official poster for the 1950 tournament.

IV CAMPEONATO
MUNDIAL DE
FUTEBOL
·TAÇA JULES RIMET·

BRASIL
JUNHO DE 1950

Groups

GROUP 1
	P	W	D	L	F	A	PTS
Brazil	3	2	1	0	8	2	5
Yugoslavia	3	2	0	1	7	3	4
Switzerland	3	1	1	1	4	6	3
Mexico	3	0	0	3	2	10	0

Brazil qualified for the final pool.

GROUP 2
	P	W	D	L	F	A	PTS
Spain	3	3	0	0	6	1	6
England	3	1	0	2	2	2	2
Chile	3	1	0	2	5	6	2
USA	3	1	0	2	4	8	2

Spain qualified for the final pool.

GROUP 3
	P	W	D	L	F	A	PTS
Sweden	2	1	1	0	5	4	3
Italy	2	1	0	1	4	3	2
Paraguay	2	0	1	1	1	4	1

Sweden qualified for the final pool. The group was reduced to three teams by the withdrawal of India. Legend has it they pulled out of the competition because FIFA insisted that they wear boots!

GROUP 4
	P	W	D	L	F	A	PTS
Uruguay	1	1	0	0	8	0	2
Bolivia	1	0	0	1	0	8	0

Uruguay qualified for the final pool. The number of teams in the group was halved by the withdrawal of Scotland, Turkey and the various countries invited to replace them.

Final Pool
Brazil, Spain, Sweden, Uruguay

9 July 1950 • Pacaembu, São Paulo • 44,802 •
Mervyn Griffiths (WAL)
URUGUAY (1) 2 Ghiggia 27, Varela 72
SPAIN (2) 2 Basora 39, 41

9 July 1950 • Maracanã, Rio de Janeiro • 138,886 •
Arthur Ellis (ENG)
BRAZIL (3) 7 Ademir 17, 37, 51, 59, Chico 39,
87, Maneca 85
SWEDEN (0) 1 Andersson pen 67

13 July 1950 • Pacaembu, São Paulo • 7,987 •
Giovanni Galeati (ITA)
URUGUAY (1) 3 Ghiggia 39, Míguez 77, 84
SWEDEN (2) 2 Palmér 4, Sundkvist 41

13 July 1950 • Maracanã, Rio de Janeiro •
152,772 • Reg Leafe (ENG)
BRAZIL (3) 6 Parra o.g. 15, Jair 21, Chico 29, 55,
Ademir 57, Zizinho 74
SPAIN (0) 1 Igoa 70

16 July 1950 • Pacaembu, São Paulo •
11,227 • Karel van der Meer (HOL)
SWEDEN (2) 3 Sundkvist 15, Mellberg 34, Palmér 79
SPAIN (0) 1 Zarra 82

16 July 1950 • Maracanã, Rio de Janeiro •
205,000 • George Reader (ENG)

URUGUAY (0) 2 Schiaffino 66, Ghiggia 79
BRAZIL (0) 1 Friaça 47

URUGUAY Máspoli, M. González, Tejera, Gambetta, Varela (c),
Rodríguez Andrade, Ghiggia, Pérez, Míguez, Schiaffino, Morán.
BRAZIL Barbosa, Augusto (c), Juvenal, Bauer, Danilo, Bigode,
Friaça, Zizinho, Ademir, Jair, Chico.

FINAL POOL	**P**	**W**	**D**	**L**	**F**	**A**	**PTS**
Uruguay	3	2	1	0	7	5	5
Brazil	3	2	0	1	14	4	4
Sweden	3	1	0	2	6	11	2
Spain	3	0	1	2	4	11	1

LEADING GOALSCORERS 1950

8	Ademir	BRZ
5	Omar Míguez	URU
4	Estanislao Basora	SPA
4	Chico	BRZ
4	Zarra	SPA
4	Alcide Ghiggia	URU

THE LIMPING MAJOR
Switzerland 1954

FIFA RETAINED the mini-league system but couldn't resist a little tinkering. Instead of each team playing all the others in the group, two were seeded and would play only the two non-seeds – and any matches drawn after 90 minutes would go to extra-time. If the sides were still level after that, the result would stand. Arbitrary and confusing. Still, at least it was the first really representative World Cup – just at a time when it didn't seem necessary. No tournament has had a stronger favourite. The Hungarians were coming.

They brought with them genuine tactical innovations: the deep-lying centre-forward, so hard to mark; the near-post crosses later copied by Ron Greenwood; a system based on moving triangles. They also introduced some of the best players in the world: Grosics in goal; the smooth Bozsik in midfield; Hidegkuti the centre-forward; Czibor on the wing; and the great front men – Kocsis so marvellous in the air, plus the incomparable Puskás – who scored 158 international goals between them. Switzerland wasn't a big enough stage.

No-one else seemed to come close, though Uruguay and Yugoslavia had several of their 1950 players and some skilful reinforcements. Brazil, their great forward trio gone, were over-compensating for their defensive frailties last time. Austria, supplanted as the best team in Europe, were in decline. West Germany had only just been allowed back into FIFA.

Groups

GROUP 1

	P	W	D	L	F	A	PTS
Brazil	2	1	1	0	6	1	3
Yugoslavia	2	1	1	0	2	1	3
France	2	1	0	1	3	3	2
Mexico	2	0	0	2	2	8	0

Brazil and Yugoslavia qualified for the quarter-finals.

GROUP 2

	P	W	D	L	F	A	PTS
Hungary	2	2	0	0	17	3	4
W. Germany	2	1	0	1	7	9	2
Turkey	2	1	0	1	8	4	2
S. Korea	2	0	0	2	0	16	0

West Germany and Turkey played off (7–2) to join Hungary in the quarter-finals.

GROUP 3

	P	W	D	L	F	A	PTS
Uruguay	2	2	0	0	9	0	4
Austria	2	2	0	0	6	0	4
Czech	2	0	0	2	0	7	0
Scotland	2	0	0	2	0	8	0

Uruguay and Austria qualified for the quarter-finals.

GROUP 4

	P	W	D	L	F	A	PTS
England	2	1	1	0	6	4	3
Italy	2	1	0	1	5	3	2
Switzerland	2	1	0	1	2	3	2
Belgium	2	0	1	1	5	8	1

Italy and Switzerland played off (1–4) to join England in the quarter-finals.

Quarter-finals

26 June 1954 • St Jakob, Basle • 28,000 •
Erich Steiner (AUT)
URUGUAY (2) 4 Borges 5, Varela 38, Schiaffino
47, Ambrois 79
ENGLAND (1) 2 Lofthouse 15, Finney 66

26 June 1954 • La Pontaise, Lausanne •
32,000 • Charlie Faultless (SCO)
AUSTRIA (5) 7 Wagner 25, 28, 54, A. Körner 26,
34, Ocwirk 32, Probst 77
SWITZERLAND (4) 5 Ballaman 16, 36, Hügi 17,
18, 60

27 June 1954 • Charmilles, Geneva • 17,000 •
István Zsolt (HUN)
WEST GERMANY (1) 2 Horvat o.g. 9, Rahn 86
YUGOSLAVIA (0) 0

27 June 1954 • Wankdorf, Berne • 40,000 •
Arthur Ellis (ENG)
HUNGARY (2) 4 Hidegkuti 4, Kocsis 7, 88,
Lantos pen 61
BRAZIL (1) 2 D. Santos pen 18, Julinho 66

Semi-finals

30 June 1954 • St Jakob, Basle • 57,000 •
Vincenzo Orlandini (ITA)

WEST GERMANY (1) 6 Schäfer 31, Morlock 47,
F. Walter pen 56, pen 65, O. Walter 62, 88
AUSTRIA (0) 1 Probst 52

W. GERMANY *Turek, Posipal, Kohlmeyer, Eckel, Liebrich, Mai,
Rahn, Morlock, O. Walter, F. Walter (c), Schäfer.*
AUSTRIA *Zeman, Hanappi, Happel, Schleger, Ocwirk (c), Koller,
R. Körner, Wagner, Stojaspal, Probst, A. Körner.*

30 June 1954 • La Pontaise, Lausanne •
45,000 • Mervyn Griffiths (WAL)

HUNGARY (1) (2) 4
Czibor 12, Hidegkuti 47, Kocsis 109, 116
URUGUAY (0) (2) 2 Hohberg 76, 87

HUNGARY *Grosics, Buzánszky, Lantos, Bozsik (c), Lóránt,
Zakariás, Budai, Kocsis, Palotás, Hidegkuti, Czibor.*
URUGUAY *Máspoli, Santamaría, Martínez (c), Rodríguez
Andrade, Carballo, Cruz, Souto, Ambrois, Schiaffino, Hohberg,
Borges.*

Opposite: The rather whimsical programme for the 1954 Final.

3rd-place Final

3 July 1954 • Hardturm, Zürich • 32,000 • Paul Wyssling (SWI)

AUSTRIA (1) 3 Stojaspal pen 15, Cruz o.g. 59, Ocwirk 78
URUGUAY (1) 1 Hohberg 21

AUSTRIA *Schmied, Hanappi, Kollmann, Barschandt, Ocwirk (c), Koller, R. Körner, Wagner, Dienst, Stojaspal, Probst.*
URUGUAY *Máspoli, Santamaría, Martínez (c), Rodríguez Andrade, Carballo, Cruz, Abbadíe, Hohberg, Méndez, Schiaffino, Borges.*

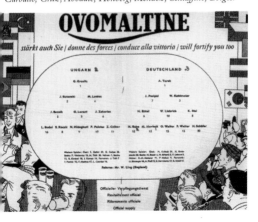

Final

4 July 1954 • Wankdorf, Berne • 62,472 •
Bill Ling (ENG)

WEST GERMANY (2) 3 Morlock 10, Rahn 19, 85
HUNGARY (2) 2 Puskás 6, Czibor 8

W. GERMANY *Turek,
Posipal, Kohlmeyer, Eckel,
Liebrich, Mai, Rahn,
Morlock, O. Walter, F. Walter
(c), Schäfer.*
HUNGARY *Grosics,
Buzánszky, Lantos, Bozsik,
Lóránt, Zakariás, Czibor,
Kocsis, Hidegkuti, Puskás (c),
M. Tóth.*

*The Hungarian squad from
1954, including Kocsis, the tournament's leading scorer.*

LEADING GOALSCORERS 1954

11	Sándor Kocsis	HUN
6	Josef Hügi	SWI
6	Erich Probst	AUT
6	Max Morlock	WG

TEENAGE KICKS

Sweden 1958

FOR THE FIRST TIME in the World Cup finals there
was no outright favourite. The hosts had as good a
chance as anyone once they recalled Raynor as coach and
broke with tradition by picking players with Italian clubs.
Liedholm, Skoglund, Hamrin and Gustavsson were some
of the greatest players of all time. But it was an elderly
team (Gren 37, Liedholm 35, Svensson 32) and home
support might not be enough.

The 1956 revolution, crushed by Moscow, deprived
Hungary of Puskás, Kocsis and Czibor, while Hidegkuti
and Bozsik were past their best. The Soviets themselves,
entering for the first time, were Olympic champions and
had the famous Yashin in goal. West Germany had Rahn
and Schäfer, a dynamic young centre-forward in Seeler and
two new heavies in Erhardt and Szymaniak, but were still
relying on Fritz Walter, now 37, as playmaker.

Brazil had an unsatisfactory European tour in 1956
and their two qualifying games against Peru ended 1-1 and
1-0. Argentina, back at long last, had won the 1957 Copa
América with some scintillating football, scoring 25 goals
in six matches – but yet again the Italians had swooped,
taking away their brilliant inside forward trio of Sivori-
Maschio-Angelillo, all later capped by Italy.

For the first and only time, all four home countries
were there, three of them affected by the Munich air crash

which killed so many of the Manchester United squad and cost Scotland their part-time manager Matt Busby, who was badly injured. Wales, eliminated by Czechoslovakia, were given a second chance when FIFA decided that Israel, blacklisted then as now by the Asian countries, couldn't be allowed to take part without playing any qualifying matches. Wales came out of the hat, won both legs 2-0, and persuaded the Italian FA to release their best-known player, giant John Charles, at the eleventh hour. England lost three players in the air crash, and things looked bleak, especially as their group included two of the fancied teams. But for Munich, England would have been one of them.

The great Garrincha goes past Hopkins in Wales' last finals match to date.

Groups

GROUP 1

	P	W	D	L	F	A	PTS
W. Germany	3	1	2	0	7	5	4
Czechoslovakia	3	1	1	1	8	4	3
N. Ireland	3	1	1	1	4	5	3
Argentina	3	1	0	2	5	10	2

Czechoslovakia and Northern Ireland played off (1–2) to join West Germany in the quarter-finals.

GROUP 2

	P	W	D	L	F	A	PTS
France	3	2	0	1	11	7	4
Yugoslavia	3	1	2	0	7	6	4
Paraguay	3	1	1	1	9	12	3
Scotland	3	0	1	2	4	6	1

France and Yugoslavia qualified for the quarter-finals.

GROUP 3

	P	W	D	L	F	A	PTS
Sweden	3	2	1	0	5	1	5
Hungary	3	1	1	1	6	3	3
Wales	3	0	3	0	2	2	3
Mexico	3	0	1	2	1	8	1

Hungary and Wales played off (1–2) to join Sweden in the quarter-finals.

GROUP 4

	P	W	D	L	F	A	PTS
Brazil	3	2	1	0	5	0	5
USSR	3	1	1	1	4	4	3
England	3	0	3	0	4	4	3
Austria	3	0	1	2	2	7	1

England and USSR played off (0–1) to join Brazil in the quarter-finals.

Quarter-finals

19 June 1958 • Rasunda, Solna, Stockholm •
31,900 • Reg Leafe (ENG)
SWEDEN (0) 2 Hamrin 49, Simonsson 88
USSR (0) 0

19 June 1958 • Idrottsparken, Norrköping • 11,800 •
Juan Gardeazábal (SPA)
FRANCE (1) 4 Wisnieski 44, Fontaine 56, 64,
Piantoni 68
NORTHERN IRELAND (0) 0

19 June 1958 • Nya Ullevi, Gothenburg • 25,923 •
Fritz Seipelt (AUT)
BRAZIL (0) 1 Pelé 73
WALES (0) 0

19 June 1958 • Malmö Stadion • 20,055 • Paul
Wyssling (SWI)
WEST GERMANY (1) 1 Rahn 12
YUGOSLAVIA (0) 0

Semi-finals

24 June 1958 • Nya Ullevi, Gothenburg • 49,471 •
István Zsolt (HUN)

SWEDEN (1) 3 Skoglund 33, Gren 80, Hamrin 87
WEST GERMANY (1) 1 Schäfer 25

SWEDEN *Svensson, Bergmark, Axbom, Börjesson, Gustavsson, Parling, Hamrin, Gren, Simonsson, Liedholm (c), Skoglund.*
W. GERMANY *Herkenrath, Stollenwerk, Juskowiak, Eckel, Erhardt, Szymaniak, Rahn, Walter, Seeler, Schäfer (c), Cieslarczyk.*
SENT OFF: *Juskowiak 58.*

24 June 1958 • Rasunda, Solna, Stockholm • 27,100 • Mervyn Griffiths (WAL)

BRAZIL (2) 5 Vavá 2, Didi 39, Pelé 52, 64, 75
FRANCE (1) 2 Fontaine 9, Piantoni 82

BRAZIL *Gylmar, de Sordi, Santos, Zito, Bellini (c), Orlando, Garrincha, Didi, Vavá, Pelé, Zagallo.*
FRANCE *Abbes, Kaelbel, Lerond, Penverne, Jonquet (c), Marcel, Wisnieski, Kopa, Fontaine, Piantoni, Vincent.*

3rd-place Final

28 June 1958 • Nya Ullevi, Gothenburg • 32,483 • Juan Brozzi (ARG)

FRANCE (3) 6 Fontaine 15, 36, 77, 89, Kopa pen 27, Douis 50
WEST GERMANY (1) 3 Cieslarczyk 17, Rahn 52, Schäfer 83

FRANCE *Abbes, Kaelbel, Lerond, Penverne (c), Lafont, Marcel, Wisnieski, Douis, Fontaine, Kopa, Vincent.*
W. GERMANY *Kwiatkowski, Stollenwerk, Schnellinger, Erhardt, Wewers, Szymaniak, Rahn, Sturm, Kelbassa, Schäfer (c), Cieslarczyk.*

Final

29 June 1958 • Rasunda, Solna • Stockholm •
49,737 • Maurice Guigue (FRA)

BRAZIL (2) 5 Vavá 9, 32, Pelé 55, 90, Zagallo 68
SWEDEN (1) 2 Liedholm 4, Simonsson 79

BRAZIL *Gylmar, D. Santos, N. Santos, Zito, Bellini (c), Orlando, Garrincha, Didi, Vavá, Pelé, Zagallo.*
SWEDEN *Svensson, Bergmark, Axbom, Börjesson, Gustavsson, Parling, Hamrin, Gren, Simonsson, Liedholm (c), Skoglund.*

Brazil win the World Cup at last, with one of their finest teams.

LEADING GOALSCORERS 1958

13	Just Fontaine	FRA
6	Helmut Rahn	WG
6	Pelé	BRZ

THE SORCERER'S APPRENTICE

Chile 1962

THE BRAZILIAN team had broken up since 1958, but had then been almost completely re-formed. Zagallo had reclaimed his place from the explosive Pepé, Vavá from the chubby-cheeked Coutinho, Pelé's supercharged partner at Santos. Didi was back from two wasted years at Real Madrid. Only the twin stoppers were missing and even they had been replaced by names from the past; Zózimo a reserve in 1958 and Mauro who'd won his first cap in 1949. The only question mark was one of age; six of the team were over 30. But Pelé was just 21 and firmly established as the best in the world. They were obvious favourites.

The USSR had won all three matches on a tour of South America the previous year but still looked rather functional. Argentina had a new manager and a more defensive style. Yugoslavia, who'd finally struck Olympic gold after losing the previous three finals, had Sekularac at his best and dangerous strikers in Galic and Jerkovic. Czechoslovakia's famous half-backs had muscled their way past Scotland in a play-off.

Spain and Italy tried to find instant success by padding their teams with foreigners. Spain picked Martínez from Paraguay, Santamaría from Uruguay and none other than Puskás, who was now 36 but had just scored another hat-trick in a European Cup final. The great Argentinian Alfredo Di Stéfano was in the squad but apparently injured. Italy had Maschio and Sivori from Argentina and Altafini (of 1958 fame) and Sormani from Brazil, which should have added up to a dazzling forward line.

England had better players than in 1958: Armfield and Wilson arguably their best ever full-backs; Charlton and Greaves up front. In the 1960–61 season they'd beaten Scotland 9-3, Spain 4-2, Italy 3-2 away, and other teams by scores of 5-2, 9-0, 5-1 and 8-0 – but all the play still went through Haynes and the impetus seemed to have gone.

As for the hosts, they had several players of international class or thereabouts, just enough to make them respectable opposition, but only in partnership with the Santiago crowd, one of the stars of the tournament.

The Brazilian team that retained the Cup.

Groups

GROUP 1

	P	W	D	L	F	A	PTS
USSR	3	2	1	0	8	5	5
Yugoslavia	3	2	0	1	8	3	4
Uruguay	3	1	0	2	4	6	2
Colombia	3	0	1	2	5	11	1

USSR and Yugoslavia qualified for the quarter-finals.

GROUP 2

	P	W	D	L	F	A	PTS
W. Germany	3	2	1	0	4	1	5
Chile	3	2	0	1	5	3	4
Italy	3	1	1	1	3	2	3
Switzerland	3	0	0	3	2	8	0

West Germany and Chile qualified for the quarter-finals.

GROUP 3

	P	W	D	L	F	A	PTS
Brazil	3	2	1	0	4	1	5
Czechoslovakia	3	1	1	1	2	3	3
Mexico	3	1	0	2	3	4	2
Spain	3	1	0	2	2	3	2

Brazil and Czechoslovakia qualified for the quarter-finals.

GROUP 4

	P	W	D	L	F	A	PTS
Hungary	3	2	1	0	8	2	5
England	3	1	1	1	4	3	3
Argentina	3	1	1	1	2	3	3
Bulgaria	3	0	1	2	1	7	1

Hungary and England qualified for the quarter-finals.

Quarter-finals

10 June 1962 • Carlos Dittborn, Arica •
17,268 • Leo Horn (HOL)
CHILE (2) 2 L. Sánchez 11, Rojas 28
USSR (1) 1 Chislenko 26

10 June 1962 • Nacional, Santiago • 63,324 •
Arturo Yamasaki (PER)
YUGOSLAVIA (0) 1 Radakovic 85
WEST GERMANY (0) 0

10 June 1962 • El Tranque, Viña del Mar • 17,736 •
Pierre Schwinte (FRA)
BRAZIL (1) 3 Garrincha 31, 59, Vavá 53
ENGLAND (1) 1 Hitchens 38

10 June 1962 • Braden Copper, Rancagua •
11,690 • Nikolai Latyshev (USR)
CZECHOSLOVAKIA (1) 1 Scherer 13
HUNGARY (0) 0

Semi-finals

13 June 1962 • Nacional, Santiago • 76,594 •
Arturo Yamasaki (PER)

BRAZIL (2) 4 Garrincha 9, 32, Vavá 48, 78
CHILE (1) 2 Toro 42, L. Sánchez pen 62

BRAZIL *Gylmar, D. Santos, N. Santos, Zito, Mauro (c), Zózimo, Garrincha, Didi, Vavá, Amarildo, Zagallo.*
CHILE *Escuti, Eyzaguirre, Rodríguez, Contreras, R. Sánchez, Rojas, Ramírez, Toro (c), Landa, Tobar, L. Sánchez.*
SENT OFF: *Landa 80, Garrincha 84.*

13 June 1962 • El Tranque, Viña del Mar • 5,890 • Gottfried Dienst (SWI)

CZECHOSLOVAKIA (0) 3 Kadraba 48, Scherer 80, pen 84
YUGOSLAVIA (0) 1 Jerkovic 68

CZECHOSLOVAKIA *Schrojf, Lála, Novák (c), Pluskal, Popluhár, Masopust, Pospíchal, Scherer, Kadraba, Kvasnák, Jelínek.*
YUGOSLAVIA *Soskic, Durkovic, Jusufi, Radakovic, Markovic, Popovic, Sijakovic, Sekularac, Jerkovic, Galic (c), Skoblar.*

3rd-place Final

16 June 1962 • Nacional, Santiago • 66,697 • Juan Gardeazábal (SPA)

CHILE (0) 1 Rojas 89
YUGOSLAVIA (0) 0

CHILE *Godoy, Eyzaguirre, Rodríguez, Cruz, R. Sánchez, Rojas, Ramírez, Toro (c), Campos, Tobar, L. Sánchez.*
YUGOSLAVIA *Soskic, Durkovic, Svinjarevic, Radakovic, Markovic, Popovic, Kovacevic, Sekularac, Jerkovic, Galic (c), Skoblar.*

Final

17 June 1962 • Nacional, Santiago • 68 679 •
Nikolai Latyshev (USR)

BRAZIL (1) 3 Amarildo 16, Zito 69, Vavá 78
CZECHOSLOVAKIA (1) 1 Masopust 14

BRAZIL *Gylmar, D. Santos, N. Santos, Zito, Mauro (c), Zózimo,
Garrincha, Didi, Vavá, Amarildo, Zagallo.*
CZECHOSLOVAKIA *Schrojf, Tichy, Novák (c), Pluskal, Popluhár,
Masopust, Pospíchal, Scherer, Kadraba, Kvasnák, Jelínek.*

*An error by Schrojf (on the ground) presents Vavá with Brazil's third goal
in the Final.*

LEADING GOALSCORERS 1962

4	Flórián Albert	HUN	
4	Valentin Ivanov	USR	
4	Garrincha	BRZ	
4	Leonel Sánchez	CHI	2 pen
4	Drazen Jerkovic	YUG	
4	Vavá	BRZ	

THE SHADOW OF A DOUBT

England 1966

MOST CERTAINLY, said Alfred Ernest Ramsey – using that famous phrase of his – most certainly England will win the World Cup. The man with a legendary aversion to the press had provided them with their juiciest quote. There it was on record, a rod for his own back.

Ramsey knew he hadn't been first choice to replace Winterbottom as manager, but no doubt thought he should have been. None of the other candidates could have achieved what he did in 1961–62, taking little Ipswich Town to the First Division title the season after bringing them out of the Second. The new man had credentials – and more power. He took the job on condition that the selection committee which had so hindered poor Winterbottom was disbanded. All team decisions would be his, bringing England into the twentieth century.

There was also the little matter of home advantage, and enough good players to fortify Sir Alf's optimism. Bobby Moore, now the captain, had matured into probably the best defender in the world and the rest of the back four looked just as dependable. Bobby Charlton had moved into midfield, where he saw more of the ball but didn't quite look the part of playmaker. Greaves recovered well enough from hepatitis to score four goals in a warm-up match.

Italy were devastating at home but far less convincing away. West Germany, who'd shown their mettle by winning in Sweden after drawing at home, had Seeler up front, new stars in midfield, and several players from the Borussia Dortmund team which had just beaten Liverpool in the Cup Winners Cup final. Argentina won the 'Little World Cup' in Brazil, beating the hosts, England and Portugal, then recalled the dreaded Lorenzo as manager. Portugal, heavily reliant on Benfica, had qualified for the first time by putting out the 1962 runners-up Czechoslovakia, the only goal in Bratislava scored by Eusébio, the European Footballer of the Year. The USSR were strong.

Meanwhile, Brazil seemed to believe the Cup was now theirs by right. All they needed was to resuscitate

some of the veterans from 1962 and even 1958. So out went the young Carlos Alberto and Djalma Dias, back came Bellini (now 36) and Orlando. In stayed Djalma Santos (37), Gylmar (35), Zito (33) and an injury-prone Garrincha. There were some promising newcomers – Jairzinho, Gérson, Tostão, the 16-year-old Edu – but their time hadn't yet come. As in 1962, Pelé was the one great hope, still very much the best in the world – but there was no Amarildo to act as deputy; he'd been dropped too. 'There is only one way to describe Brazil's 1966 World Cup effort and that is to openly declare that from the beginning it was a total and unmitigated disaster.' Pelé's words – and England fans wanted to believe them.

Groups

GROUP 1	P	W	D	L	F	A	PTS
England	3	2	1	0	4	0	5
Uruguay	3	1	2	0	2	1	4
Mexico	3	0	2	1	1	3	2
France	3	0	1	2	2	5	1

England and Uruguay qualified for the quarter-finals.

GROUP 2	P	W	D	L	F	A	PTS
W. Germany	3	2	1	0	7	1	5
Argentina	3	2	1	0	4	1	5
Spain	3	1	0	2	4	5	2
Switzerland	3	0	0	3	1	9	0

West Germany and Argentina qualified for the quarter-finals.

GROUP 3	**P**	**W**	**D**	**L**	**F**	**A**	**PTS**
Portugal	3	3	0	0	9	2	6
Hungary	3	2	0	1	7	5	4
Brazil	3	1	0	2	4	6	2
Bulgaria	3	0	0	3	1	8	0

Portugal and Hungary qualified for the quarter-finals.

GROUP 4	**P**	**W**	**D**	**L**	**F**	**A**	**PTS**
USSR	3	3	0	0	6	1	6
N. Korea	3	1	1	1	2	4	3
Italy	3	1	0	2	2	2	2
Chile	3	0	1	2	2	5	1

USSR and North Korea qualified for the quarter-finals.

Quarter-finals

23 July 1966 • Wembley, London • 90,584 •
Rudolf Kreitlein (WG)
ENGLAND (0) 1 Hurst 77
ARGENTINA (0) 0

23 July 1966 • Hillsborough, Sheffield • 40,007 •
Jim Finney (ENG)
WEST GERMANY (1) 4 Haller 11, 84,
Beckenbauer 70, Seeler 77
URUGUAY (0) 0

23 July 1966 • Goodison Park, Liverpool • 40,248 •
Menachem Ashkenazi (ISR)
PORTUGAL (2) 5 Eusébio 26, pen 43, 57, pen 60,
José Augusto 80
NORTH KOREA (3) 3 Park Seung-jin 1, Lee Dong-
woon 20, Yang Sung-kook 24

23 July 1966 • Roker Park, Sunderland • 22,103 •
Juan Gardeazábal (SPA)
USSR (1) 2 Chislenko 5, Porkujan 48
HUNGARY (0) 1 Bene 58

Semi-finals

25 July 1966 • Goodison Park, Liverpool • 38,273 •
Concetto Lo Bello (ITA)

WEST GERMANY (1) 2 Haller 43, Beckenbauer 68
USSR (0) 1 Porkujan 87

W. GERMANY *Tilkowski, Lutz, Schnellinger, Beckenbauer,
Schulz, Weber, Held, Haller, Seeler (c), Overath, Emmerich.*
USSR *Yashin, Ponomaryev, Shesternev (c), Danilov, Voronin,
Sabo, Khusainov, Chislenko, Banishevsky, Malofeyev, Porkujan.*
SENT OFF: *Chislenko 44.*

26 July 1966 • Wembley, London • 94,493 • Pierre Schwinte (FRA)

ENGLAND (1) 2 R. Charlton 30, 79
PORTUGAL (0) 1 Eusébio pen 82

ENGLAND *Banks, Cohen, Wilson, Stiles, J. Charlton, Moore (c), Ball, Hurst, R. Charlton, Hunt, Peters.*
PORTUGAL *Pereira, Festa, Baptista, Graça, José Carlos, Hilário, José Augusto, Coluna (c), Torres, Eusébio, Simões.*

3rd-place Final

28 July 1966 • Wembley, London • 87,696 • Ken Dagnall (ENG)

PORTUGAL (1) 2 Eusébio pen 13, Torres 88
USSR (1) 1 Malofeyev 44

PORTUGAL *Pereira, Festa, Baptista, Graça, José Carlos, Hilário, José Augusto, Coluna (c), Torres, Eusébio, Simões.*
USSR *Yashin (c), Ponomaryev, Korneyev, Sichinava, Khurtsilava, Danilov, Serebrianikov, Voronin, Banishevsky, Malofeyev, Metreveli.*

LEADING GOALSCORERS 1966

9	Eusébio	POR	4 pen.
6	Helmut Haller	WG	1 pen.
4	Ferenc Bene	HUN	
4	Franz Beckenbauer	WG	
4	Valery Porkujan	USR	
4	Geoff Hurst	ENG	

Final

30 July 1966 • Wembley, London • 93,802 •
Gottfried Dienst (SWI)

ENGLAND (1) (2) 4 Hurst 19, 100, 119, Peters 78
WEST GERMANY (1) (2) 2 Haller 13, Weber 89

ENGLAND *Banks, Cohen, Wilson, Stiles, J. Charlton, Moore (c),
Ball, Hurst, R. Charlton, Hunt, Peters.*
W. GERMANY *Tilkowski, Höttges, Schnellinger, Beckenbauer,
Schulz, Weber, Held, Haller, Seeler (c), Overath, Emmerich.*

*30 July 1966. Wilson struggles to uphold Moore, who has no such trouble
with the gold statuette.*

THE HEIGHT OF BRILLIANCE: 7,000 FEET

Mexico 1970

IN THE FOUR years between World Cups, Ramsey's England lost just four out of 35 matches, only against very good teams and never by more than one goal. Banks, Moore, Ball, Hurst, Peters and the Charltons were still there, and Stiles had been replaced by Mullery, who was better on the ball and almost as spiky off it. There was a dynamic new winger in Lee and an excellent crop of attacking full-backs, increasingly necessary in a wingless team.

But they weren't the favourites. Brazil had done enough to serve notice that 1966 was firmly behind them and had a powerful team including Tostão, whose promise was now being fulfilled in a rich partnership with a rejuvenated Pelé; Carlos Alberto, Gérson and Jairzinho, all coming into their prime; and new blood in Clodoaldo and Rivelino.

Elsewhere, West Germany added the great goalscoring talents of Gerd Müller to their 1966 squad but scraped through the qualifiers. Italy looked strong. Argentina, more violent than ever, were eliminated by Peru despite almost unlimited injury-time in the deciding match. The USSR put out a Northern Ireland team denied the services of George Best. And Mexico's position as hosts allowed another Central American country to take part, El Salvador qualifying after three matches with neighbouring Honduras.

FIFA turned a blind eye to the enormous problems of heat and altitude which had left European competitors needing oxygen at the Olympic Games. Indeed, they added to them by arranging matches at noon to accommodate European television schedules. While FIFA fiddled, players burned, losing ten pounds in fluid during a single game or being sent home with heatstroke. The tournament produced some exhilarating football, and one of the greatest forward lines, but the price, in human terms, was a rip-off.

The winning team from 1970 – Brazil take the trophy again.

Groups

GROUP 1	P	W	D	L	F	A	PTS
USSR	3	2	1	0	6	1	5
Mexico	3	2	1	0	5	0	5
Belgium	3	1	0	2	4	5	2
El Salvador	3	0	0	3	0	9	0

USSR and Mexico qualified for the quarter-finals.

GROUP 2

	P	W	D	L	F	A	PTS
Italy	3	1	2	0	1	0	4
Uruguay	3	1	1	1	2	1	3
Sweden	3	1	1	1	2	2	3
Israel	3	0	2	1	1	3	1

Italy and Uruguay qualified for the quarter-finals. Italy set a record by winning their group despite scoring only a single goal.

GROUP 3

	P	W	D	L	F	A	PTS
Brazil	3	3	0	0	8	3	6
England	3	2	0	1	2	1	4
Romania	3	1	0	2	4	5	2
Czechoslovakia	3	0	0	3	2	7	0

Brazil and England qualified for the quarter-finals.

GROUP 4

	P	W	D	L	F	A	PTS
W. Germany	3	3	0	0	10	4	6
Peru	3	2	0	1	7	5	4
Bulgaria	3	0	1	2	5	9	1
Morocco	3	0	1	2	2	6	1

West Germany and Peru qualified for the quarter-finals.

Quarter-finals

14 June 1970 • Azteca, Mexico City • 96,085 •
Laurens van Ravens (HOL)
URUGUAY (0) (0) 1 Espárrago 117
USSR (0) (0) 0

14 June 1970 • Luis Gutiérrez Dosal, Toluca •
26,851 • Rudi Scheurer (SWI)
ITALY (1) 4 Guzmán o.g. 25, Riva 63, 76, Rivera 70
MEXICO (1) 1 González 13

14 June 1970 • Jalisco, Guadalajara • 54,233 •
Vital Loraux (BEL)
BRAZIL (2) 4 Rivelino 11, Tostão 15, 52,
Jairzinho 75
PERU (1) 2 Gallardo 27, Cubillas 69

14 June 1970 • Guanajuato, León • 23,357 •
Angel Norberto Coerezza (ARG)
WEST GERMANY (0) (2) 3 Beckenbauer 67,
Seeler 82, Müller 109
ENGLAND (1) (2) 2 Mullery 32, Peters 50

Semi-finals

17 June 1970 • Jalisco, Guadalajara • 51,261•
José María Ortíz de Mendibil (SPA)

BRAZIL (1) 3 Clodoaldo 44, Jairzinho 69,
Rivelino 89
URUGUAY (1) 1 Cubilla 17

BRAZIL *Félix, Carlos Alberto (c), Everaldo, Clodoaldo, Brito,
Piazza, Jairzinho, Gérson, Tostão, Pelé, Rivelino.*
URUGUAY *Mazurkiewicz, Ancheta, Matosas, Montero Castillo,
Ubiña (c), Mújica, Cubilla, Cortés, Maneiro [Espárrago 74],
Morales, Fontes.*

17 June 1970 • Azteca, Mexico City •
102,444 • Arturo Yamasaki (MEX)

ITALY (1) (1) 4 Boninsegna 8, Burgnich 98,
Riva 104, Rivera 111
WEST GERMANY (0) (1) 3 Schnellinger 90,
Müller 94, 110

ITALY *Albertosi, Burgnich, Facchetti (c), Bertini, Rosato [Poletti 91], Cera, Domenghini, Mazzola, [Rivera HT], Boninsegna, De Sisti, Riva.*
W. GERMANY *Maier, Vogts, Patzke [Held 65], Beckenbauer, Schnellinger, Schulz, Grabowski, Seeler (c), Müller, Overath, Löhr [Libuda 51].*

3rd-place Final

20 June 1970 • Azteca, Mexico City •
104,403 • Antonio Sbardella (ITA)

WEST GERMANY (1) 1 Overath 26
URUGUAY (0) 0

W. GERMANY *Wolter, Vogts, Schnellinger [Lorenz HT], Patzke, Fichtel, Weber, Libuda [Löhr 73], Seeler (c), Müller, Overath, Held.*
URUGUAY *Mazurkiewicz, Ancheta, Matosas, Montero Castillo, Ubiña (c), Mújica, Cubilla, Cortés, Maneiro [Sandoval 67], Morales, Fontes [Espárrago HT].*

Opposite: Burgnich looks back in anguish as Pelé celebrates his goal in the 1970 Final.

Final

21 June 1970 • Azteca, Mexico City •
107,412 • Rudi Glöckner (EG)

BRAZIL (1) 4 Pelé 18, Gérson 66, Jairzinho 71,
Carlos Alberto 86
ITALY (1) 1 Boninsegna 37

BRAZIL *Félix, Carlos Alberto (c), Everaldo, Clodoaldo, Brito,
Piazza, Jairzinho, Gérson, Tostão, Pelé, Rivelino.*
ITALY *Albertosi, Burgnich, Facchetti (c), Bertini [Juliano 74],
Rosato, Cera, Domenghini, Mazzola, Boninsegna [Rivera 84],
De Sisti, Riva.*

LEADING GOALSCORERS 1970

10	Gerd Müller	WG	1 pen
7	Jairzinho	BRZ	
5	Teófilo Cubillas	PER	

ORANGE IS NOT THE ONLY FRUIT

West Germany 1974

BRAZIL LOST the World Cup almost as soon as they regained it. The Jules Rimet Trophy, theirs to keep after they'd won it for the third time, was stolen and never seen again. Their 1970 team melted away too, Pelé retiring too early at 31 and three important players dropping out injured: Carlos Alberto, Clodoaldo and especially Tostão, whose eye problem had resurfaced. In their absence, Zagallo put together a far more physical side, in the belief that the old skills wouldn't survive against European athleticism.

No-one seemed to epitomize this more than the hosts and favourites, who'd won the 1972 European Championship with some masterly all-round football. Three of the team finished 1-2-3 in the European Footballer of the Year poll and there were world-class players in every department: Maier in goal; Vogts and the new discovery Breitner at full-back; the incomparable Beckenbauer, now the world's first great attacking sweeper; the imperious blond Netzer in midfield; Müller ever more unstoppable up front.

Italy were as defensive as ever and apparently even more impregnable. Zoff had just completed 12 consecutive internationals without conceding a goal. But they were an ageing team, short of goalscoring power. Scotland were back for the first time since 1958, good in parts but lacking a genuine midfield general. Holland still hadn't harnessed the brilliance of their Ajax players, who'd just been beaten in the European Cup after winning it three years in a row.

Yet again FIFA couldn't leave well alone. Although the format of the last three tournaments had been generally acceptable, they insisted on trying to give the event more of the appearance of a league and making the successful teams play an extra match, as if that would give the winners more credibility as World Champions. All it succeeded in doing was tiring the players even more and depriving spectators of two knockout rounds. All for a few dollars more.

Above: Johan Cruyff had the football world at his feet – until the 1974 Final.

Groups

GROUP 1

	P	W	D	L	F	A	PTS
E. Germany	3	2	1	0	4	1	5
W. Germany	3	2	0	1	4	1	4
Chile	3	0	2	1	1	2	2
Australia	3	0	1	2	0	5	1

East Germany and West Germany qualified for the second round.

GROUP 2

	P	W	D	L	F	A	PTS
Yugoslavia	3	1	2	0	10	1	4
Brazil	3	1	2	0	3	0	4
Scotland	3	1	2	0	3	1	4
Zaire	3	0	0	3	0	14	0

Yugoslavia and Brazil qualified for the second round.

GROUP 3

	P	W	D	L	F	A	PTS
Holland	3	2	1	0	6	1	5
Sweden	3	1	2	0	3	0	4
Bulgaria	3	0	2	1	2	5	2
Uruguay	3	0	1	2	1	6	1

Holland and Sweden qualified for the second round.

GROUP 4

	P	W	D	L	F	A	PTS
Poland	3	3	0	0	12	3	6
Argentina	3	1	1	1	7	5	3
Italy	3	1	1	1	5	4	3
Haiti	3	0	0	3	2	14	0

Poland and Argentina qualified for the second round.

2ND ROUND

Group A
Argentina, Brazil, East Germany, Holland

26 June 1974 • Niedersachsen, Hanover • 58,463 •
Clive Thomas (WAL)
BRAZIL (0) 1 Rivelino 60
EAST GERMANY (0) 0

26 June 1974 • Parkstadion, Gelsenkirchen •
55,348 • Bobby Davidson (SCO)
HOLLAND (2) 4 Cruyff 11, 90, Krol 25,
Rep 73
ARGENTINA (0) 0

*The 1974 Dutch team. (l-r)
Neeskens, Krol, van
Hanegem, Jansen, Suurbier,
Rep, Rijsbergen, Rensenbrink,
Haan, Jongbloed, Cruyff.*

30 June 1974 • Parkstadion, Gelsenkirchen •
67,148 • Rudi Scheurer (SWI)
HOLLAND (1) 2 Neeskens 7, Rensenbrink 59
EAST GERMANY (0) 0

30 June 1974 • Niedersachsen, Hanover • 38,000 •
Vital Loraux (BEL)
BRAZIL (1) 2 Rivelino 32, Jairzinho 49
ARGENTINA (1) 1 Brindisi 35

3 July 1974 • Parkstadion, Gelsenkirchen • 53,054 •
Jack Taylor (ENG)
ARGENTINA (1) 1 Houseman 20
EAST GERMANY (1) 1 Streich 14

3 July 1974 • Westfalen, Dortmund • 52,500 • Kurt
Tschenscher (WG)
HOLLAND (0) 2 Neeskens 50, Cruyff 65
BRAZIL (0) 0

GROUP A	**P**	**W**	**D**	**L**	**F**	**A**	**PTS**
Holland	3	3	0	0	6	0	6
Brazil	3	2	0	1	3	3	4
E. Germany	3	0	1	2	1	4	1
Argentina	3	0	1	2	2	7	1

Holland qualified for the Final, Brazil for the 3rd-place Final.

Group B
Poland, Sweden, West Germany, Yugoslavia

26 June 1974 • Rheinstadion, Düsseldorf • 66,085 •
Armando Marques (BRZ)
WEST GERMANY (1) 2 Breitner 39, Müller 82
YUGOSLAVIA (0) 0

26 June 1974 • Neckar, Stuttgart • 43,755 •
Ramón Barreto (URU)
POLAND (1) 1 Lato 43
SWEDEN (0) 0

30 June 1974 • Waldstadion, Frankfurt • 53,200 •
Rudi Glöckner (EG)
POLAND (1) 2 Deyna pen 24, Lato 62
YUGOSLAVIA (1) 1 Karasi 43

30 June 1974 • Rheinstadion, Düsseldorf • 67,861 •
Pavel Kasakov (USR)
WEST GERMANY (0) 4 Overath 51, Bonhof 52,
Grabowski 76, Hoeness, pen 89
SWEDEN (1) 2 Edström 24, Sandberg 53

3 July 1974 • Waldstadion, Frankfurt • 61,249 •
Erich Linemayr (AUT)
WEST GERMANY (0) 1 Müller 76
POLAND (0) 0

3 July 1974 • Rheinstadion, Düsseldorf •
37,700 • Luis Pestarino (ARG)
SWEDEN (1) 2 Edström 29, Torstensson 85
YUGOSLAVIA (1) 1 Surjak 27

GROUP B	P	W	D	L	F	A	PTS
W. Germany	3	3	0	0	7	2	6
Poland	3	2	0	1	3	2	4
Sweden	3	1	0	2	4	6	2
Yugoslavia	3	0	0	3	2	6	0

*West Germany qualified for the Final, Poland for the
3rd-place Final.*

3rd-place Final

6 July 1974 • Olympia, Munich • 74,100 • Aurelio Angonese (ITA)

POLAND (0) 1 Lato 76
BRAZIL (0) 0

POLAND *Tomaszewski, Szymanowski, Musial, Maszczyk, Gorgon, Zmuda, Lato, Kasperczak [Cmikiewicz 73], Szarmach [Kapka 73], Deyna (c), Gadocha.*
BRAZIL *Leão, Zé Maria, Marinho Chagas, Carpegiani, Alfredo, Marinho Peres (c), Valdomiro, Ademir da Guia [Mirandinha 66], Jairzinho, Rivelino, Dirceu.*

Final

7 July 1974 • Olympia, Munich • 77,833 • Jack Taylor (ENG)

WEST GERMANY (2) 2 Breitner pen 25, Müller 43
HOLLAND (1) 1 Neeskens pen 2

W. GERMANY *Maier, Vogts, Breitner, Bonhof, Schwarzenbeck, Beckenbauer (c), Grabowski, Hoeness, Müller, Overath, Hölzenbein.*
HOLLAND *Jongbloed, Suurbier, Krol, Jansen, Rijsbergen [de Jong 68], Haan, Rep, Neeskens, van Hanegem, Cruyff (c), Rensenbrink [R. van de Kerkhof HT].*

LEADING GOALSCORERS 1974

7	Grzegorz Lato	POL	
5	Andrzej Szarmach	POL	
5	Johan Neeskens	HOL	3 pen.

THE LAST POST

Argentina 1978

I T WAS ABOUT time Argentina hosted the main event. They'd applied for it in the past and were one of the major footballing powers, so no-one had many qualms when they were awarded the 1978 tournament. Doubts and reservations about the effects on the tournament of the new military government that had seized power were swept aside and the junta, deeply in need of a public relations coup, spent the vast sums required to build three new stadia and police the event thoroughly. It passed without much incident off the pitch, but at a cost in more ways than one.

Of the competing countries, several looked strong in parts. The holders had replaced several of their 1974 team with some talented newcomers but were without Beckenbauer, who'd opted to pick up some easy money in the USA. Unable to find a replacement, West Germany were using Manni Kaltz, a big attacking right-back, as their sweeper.

If any player was missed even more than the Kaiser, it was Cruyff, who'd simply had enough of life in the goldfish bowl. And van Hanegem dropped out when he couldn't be guaranteed a place in the starting line-up. But Holland retained many of the 1974 side and looked the strongest of the European challengers. Italy, trying to assimilate the attacking philosophy of a new coach, had beaten an England team with several well-known names (Keegan, Brooking, Channon, Bowles, Hughes) but who were devoid of plan or leadership. For the second successive time, England didn't reach the finals.

Brazil, despite a different coach, were just as physical as in 1974. Argentina, like Italy, were trying to go the other way, their coach using two wingers and refusing to pick players from Lorenzo's brutal Boca Juniors. Evolution had been slow, but home advantage would surely count for something.

It was an open field, and several respected judges, including Rinus Michels and Miljan Miljanic, had a fancy for Scotland, where there seemed to be no shortage of international class: Buchan and Burns at the back; a midfield of Masson the playmaker and Rioch the destroyer who could pass; Jordan to win the ball up front for Dalglish; dribbling left-wingers in John Robertson and the recalled Willie Johnston. Enough to make people believe the voluble new manager when he intimated that Scotland's third match, against Holland, would be to decide who finished top of the group. Before that, only an ageing Peru followed by Iran, who must have been terrified to hear 'my name is Ally MacLeod and I am a born winner'.

Kenny Dalglish volleys Scotland's first goal in their surprise win over Holland.

Groups

GROUP 1

	P	W	D	L	F	A	PTS
Italy	3	3	0	0	6	2	6
Argentina	3	2	0	1	4	3	4
France	3	1	0	2	5	5	2
Hungary	3	0	0	3	3	8	0

Italy and Argentina qualified for the second round.

GROUP 2

	P	W	D	L	F	A	PTS
Poland	3	2	1	0	4	1	5
W. Germany	3	1	2	0	6	0	4
Tunisia	3	1	1	1	3	2	3
Mexico	3	0	0	3	2	12	0

Poland and West Germany qualified for the second round.

GROUP 3

	P	W	D	L	F	A	PTS
Austria	3	2	0	1	3	2	4
Brazil	3	1	2	0	2	1	4
Spain	3	1	1	1	2	2	3
Sweden	3	0	1	2	1	3	1

Austria and Brazil qualified for the second round.

GROUP 4

	P	W	D	L	F	A	PTS
Peru	3	2	1	0	7	2	5
Holland	3	1	1	1	5	3	3
Scotland	3	1	1	1	5	6	3
Iran	3	0	1	2	2	8	1

Peru and Holland qualified for the second round.

2ND ROUND
Group A
Austria, Holland, Italy, West Germany

14 June 1978 • Monumental, Buenos Aires •
67,547 • Dusan Maksimovic (YUG)
ITALY 0
WEST GERMANY 0

14 June 1978 • Chateau Carreras, Córdoba •
25,059 • John Gordon (SCO)
HOLLAND (3) 5 Brandts 6, Rensenbrink pen 35,
Rep 36, 53, W. van de Kerkhof 82
AUSTRIA (0) 1 Obermayer 80

18 June 1978 • Chateau Carreras, Córdoba •
40,750 • Ramón Barreto (URU)
HOLLAND (1) 2 Haan 27, R. van de, Kerkhof 82
WEST GERMANY (1) 2 Abramczik 3, D. Müller 70

18 June 1978 • Monumental, Buenos Aires •
40,000 • Francis Rion (BEL)
ITALY (1) 1 Rossi 13
AUSTRIA (0) 0

21 June 1978 • Chateau Carreras, Córdoba •
38,318 • Avraham Klein (ISR)
AUSTRIA (0) 3 Vogts o.g. 59, Krankl 66, 88
WEST GERMANY (1) 2 Rummenigge 19,
Hölzenbein 67

21 June 1978 • Monumental, Buenos Aires •
67,433 • Angel Martínez (SPA)
HOLLAND (0) 2 Brandts 49, Haan 76
ITALY (1) 1 Brandts o.g. 19

GROUP A	P	W	D	L	F	A	PTS
Holland	3	2	1	0	9	4	5
Italy	3	1	1	1	2	2	3
W. Germany	3	0	2	1	4	5	2
Austria	3	1	0	2	4	8	2

Holland qualified for the Final, Italy for the 3rd-place Final.

Group B
Argentina, Brazil, Peru, Poland

14 June 1978 • San Martín, Mendoza •
31,278 • Nicolae Rainea (ROM)
BRAZIL (2) 3 Dirceu 15, 27, Zico pen 72
PERU (0) 0

14 June 1978 • Cordiviola, Rosario • 37,091 • Ulf
Eriksson (SWE)
ARGENTINA (1) 2 Kempes 16, 72
POLAND (0) 0

18 June 1978 • San Martín, Mendoza •
35,288 • Pat Partridge (ENG)
POLAND (0) 1 Szarmach 64
PERU (0) 0

18 June 1978 • Cordiviola, Rosario • 37,326 •
Károly Palotai (HUN)
ARGENTINA 0
BRAZIL 0

21 June 1978 • San Martín, Mendoza •
39,586 • Juan Silvagno (CHI)
BRAZIL (1) 3 Nelinho 13, Roberto Dinamite 58, 63
POLAND (1) 1 Lato 45

21 June 1978 • Cordiviola, Rosario • 37,326 •
Robert Wurtz (FRA)
ARGENTINA (2) 6 Kempes 21, 49, Tarantini 43,
Luque 50, 72, Houseman 67
PERU (0) 0

GROUP B	**P**	**W**	**D**	**L**	**F**	**A**	**PTS**
Argentina	3	2	1	0	8	0	5
Brazil	3	2	1	0	6	1	5
Poland	3	1	0	2	2	5	2
Peru	3	0	0	3	0	10	0

Argentina qualified for the Final, Brazil for the 3rd-place Final.

3rd-place Final

24 June 1978 • Monumental, Buenos Aires •
69,659 • Avraham Klein (ISR)

BRAZIL (0) 2 Nelinho 64, Dirceu 71
ITALY (1) 1 Causio 38

BRAZIL *Leão (c), Nelinho, Rodrigues Neto, Batista, Oscar,
Amaral, Gil [Reinaldo HT], Cerezo [Rivelino 64], Roberto
Dinamite, Mendonça, Dirceu.*
ITALY *Zoff (c), Cuccureddu, Cabrini, P. Sala, Gentile, Scirea,
Causio, Maldera, Rossi, Antognoni [C. Sala 78], Bettega.*

Final

25 June 1978 • Monumental, Buenos Aires •
76,609 • Sergio Gonella (ITA)

ARGENTINA (1) (1) 3 Kempes 37, 104,
Bertoni 115
HOLLAND (0) (1) 1 Nanninga 82

ARGENTINA *Fillol, Olguin, Tarantini, Gallego, Galván,
Passarella (c), Bertoni, Ardiles [Larrosa 65], Luque, Kempes,
Ortíz [Houseman 74].*
HOLLAND *Jongbloed, Krol (c), Brandts, Poortvliet, Jansen
[Suurbier 72], Haan, R. van de Kerkhof, Neeskens, Rep
[Nanninga 59], W. van de Kerkhof, Rensenbrink.*

LEADING GOALSCORERS 1978

6	Mario Kempes	ARG	
5	Teófilo Cubillas	PER	2 pen
5	Rob Rensenbrink	HOL	4 pen

A blizzard of tickertape, one of the abiding memories of Argentina '78.

ROSSI FIXES IT

Spain 1982

NOT FOR the first or last time, FIFA insisted on tampering with the format. Still trying to breed a successful cross between league and cup, they came up with even more of a camel. The top two teams in each group would go into four groups of three, the winners progressing to the semi-finals. There were now 24 countries instead of 16, including an increase in the number of finalists from Africa, Asia and Central America.

The champions Argentina came with the same coach and many of the same players from 1978, plus one special newcomer, the stocky Maradona, who'd been left out of the previous finals only because Menotti thought him too young and vulnerable at 17 (he'd first capped him at 16). Now he looked the world's greatest player since Cruyff or even Pelé, a target for Barcelona and every defender in the tournament.

West Germany, who'd thrown out the old wood, were the European Champions and had won all eight qualifiers with a goal tally of 33-3. Rummenigge was now a front player of the highest class and there were formidable new defenders in Briegel, Stielike and Karlheinz Förster, but their blond young playmaker Bernd Schuster was out injured.

Italy hadn't looked altogether convincing in qualifying, but at least Rossi was back after serving a suspension of less than two years for his involvement in a major match-fixing scandal. The defence was better than ever and the whole team had been together for four more years. Spain, whose national team rarely matched the success of their club sides, were cursed with unexceptional players just when their time came to host the tournament.

Three of the British Isles countries had qualified and the other two came close. The Republic of Ireland were unfortunate to finish a very close third in a strong group which saw Holland eliminated. Wales beat Czechoslovakia but were undone by a draw with Iceland in Swansea, where the floodlights failed. England had made

their fans ride a remarkable rollercoaster. Defeats in Romania and Switzerland were followed by a convincing win in Hungary and another defeat, strangest of all, in Norway ('Your boys took a helluva beating!'). But Switzerland won in Romania to let them through, after which they put together an unbeaten run, though injuries to Brooking and the talismanic Keegan were a worry.

Above: Maradona's first World Cup ends with a sending-off against Brazil. Tarantini offers consolation.

Northern Ireland, under their benign but pragmatic manager Billy Bingham, who'd played in the 1958 finals, came second in a group won by Scotland, who'd replaced MacLeod with the unimpeachable figure of Jock Stein. Although they scored only nine goals in eight qualifying games, their attack looked better than that and at last there was some organization at the back.

Brazil, under a new coach, were looking their old selves again, a very passable impersonation of the 1970 team: thin in defence, explosively brilliant everywhere else. They'd beaten England at Wembley and in their last match before the finals had thrashed the Republic of Ireland 7-0. The 'beautiful game' was back and the rest of the field would be hoping to admire it at a distance for as long as possible.

Groups

GROUP 1	P	W	D	L	F	A	PTS
Poland	3	1	2	0	5	1	4
Italy	3	0	3	0	2	2	3
Cameroon	3	0	3	0	1	1	3
Peru	3	0	2	1	2	6	2

Poland and Italy qualified for the second round.

GROUP 2	P	W	D	L	F	A	PTS
W. Germany	3	2	0	1	6	3	4
Austria	3	2	0	1	3	1	4
Algeria	3	2	0	1	5	5	4
Chile	3	0	0	3	3	8	0

West Germany and Austria qualified for the second round.

GROUP 3

	P	W	D	L	F	A	PTS
Belgium	3	2	1	0	3	1	5
Argentina	3	2	0	1	6	2	4
Hungary	3	1	1	1	12	6	3
El Salvador	3	0	0	3	1	13	0

Belgium and Argentina qualified for the second round.

GROUP 4

	P	W	D	L	F	A	PTS
England	3	3	0	0	6	1	6
France	3	1	1	1	6	5	3
Czechoslovakia	3	0	2	1	2	4	2
Kuwait	3	0	1	2	2	6	1

England and France qualified for the second round.

GROUP 5

	P	W	D	L	F	A	PTS
N. Ireland	3	1	2	0	2	1	4
Spain	3	1	1	1	3	3	3
Yugoslavia	3	1	1	1	2	2	3
Honduras	3	0	2	1	2	3	2

Northern Ireland and Spain qualified for the second round.

GROUP 6

	P	W	D	L	F	A	PTS
Brazil	3	3	0	0	10	2	6
USSR	3	1	1	1	6	4	3
Scotland	3	1	1	1	8	8	3
N. Zealand	3	0	0	3	2	12	0

Brazil and USSR qualified for the second round.

2ND ROUND

Group A
Belgium, Poland, USSR

28 June 1982 • Nou Camp, Barcelona •
30,000 • Luis Siles (COS)
POLAND (2) 3 Boniek 4, 27, 53
BELGIUM (0) 0

1 July 1982 • Nou Camp, Barcelona • 25,000 •
Michel Vautrot (FRA)
USSR (0) 1 Oganesian 49
BELGIUM (0) 0

4 July 1982 • Nou Camp, Barcelona • 45,000 •
Bob Valentine (SCO)
POLAND 0
USSR 0

GROUP A	P	W	D	L	F	A	PTS
Poland	2	1	1	0	3	0	3
USSR	2	1	1	0	1	0	3
Belgium	2	0	0	2	0	4	0

Poland qualified for the semi-finals.

Group B
England, Spain, West Germany

29 June 1982 • Bernabéu, Madrid • 75,000 •
Arnaldo Coelho (BRZ)
ENGLAND 0
WEST GERMANY 0

2 July 1982 • Bernabéu, Madrid • 90,089 •
Paolo Casarin (ITA)
WEST GERMANY (0) 2 Littbarski 50, Fischer 76
SPAIN (0) 1 Zamora 83

5 July 1982 • Bernabéu, Madrid • 65,000 •
Alexis Ponnet (BEL)
ENGLAND 0
SPAIN 0

GROUP B	P	W	D	L	F	A	PTS
W. Germany	2	1	1	0	2	1	3
England	2	0	2	0	0	0	2
Spain	2	0	1	1	1	2	1

West Germany qualified for the semi-finals.

Group C
Argentina, Brazil, Italy

29 June 1982 • Sarriá, Barcelona • 39,000 •
Nicolae Rainea (ROM)
ITALY (0) 2 Tardelli 57, Cabrini 67
ARGENTINA (0) 1 Passarella 83

2 July 1982 • Sarriá, Barcelona • 44,000 •
Mario Rubio Vázquez (MEX)
BRAZIL (1) 3 Zico 12, Serginho 68, Júnior 74
ARGENTINA (0) 1 Díaz 89

5 July 1982 • Sarriá, Barcelona • 44,000 •
Avraham Klein (ISR)
ITALY (2) 3 Rossi 5, 25, 74
BRAZIL (1) 2 Sócrates 12, Falcão 68

GROUP C	P	W	D	L	F	A	PTS
Italy	2	2	0	0	5	3	4
Brazil	2	1	0	1	5	4	2
Argentina	2	0	0	2	2	5	0

Italy qualified for the semi-finals.

Group D
Austria, France, Northern Ireland

28 June 1982 • Vicente Calderón, Madrid • 30,000 •
Károly Palotai (HUN)
FRANCE (1) 1 Genghini 39
AUSTRIA (0) 0

1 July 1982 • Vicente Calderón, Madrid • 24,000 •
Adolf Prokop (EG)
AUSTRIA (0) 2 Pezzey 53, Hintermaier 67
NORTHERN IRELAND (1) 2 Hamilton 28, 74

4 July 1982 • Vicente Calderón, Madrid • 30,000 •
Alojzy Jarguz (POL)
FRANCE (1) 4 Giresse 33, 80, Rocheteau 46, 68
NORTHERN IRELAND (0) 1 Armstrong 75

GROUP D	P	W	D	L	F	A	PTS
France	2	2	0	0	5	1	4
Austria	2	0	1	1	2	3	1
N. Ireland	2	0	1	1	3	6	1

France qualified for the semi-finals.

Semi-finals

8 July 1982 • Nou Camp, Barcelona • 55,000 •
Juan Cardellino (URU)

ITALY (1) 2 Rossi 22, 73
POLAND (0) 0

ITALY Zoff (c), Bergomi, Cabrini, Tardelli, Collovati, Scirea, Oriali, Conti, Rossi, Antognoni [Marini 28], Graziani [Altobelli 70].
POLAND Mlynarczyk, Dziuba, Majewski, Janas, Zmuda (c), Matysik, Kupcewicz, Buncol, Lato, Ciolek [Palasz HT], Smolarek [Kusto 77].

LEADING GOALSCORERS 1982

6	Paolo Rossi	ITA
5	Karl-Heinz Rummenigge	WG
4	Zbigniew Boniek	POL
4	Zico	BRZ

8 July 1982 • Sánchez Pizjuán, Seville •
71,000 • Charles Corver (HOL)

WEST GERMANY (1) (1) 3
Littbarski 18, Rummenigge 103, Fischer 108
FRANCE (1) (1) 3 Platini pen 27, Trésor 93, Giresse 99
West Germany 5-4 pens.

W. GERMANY *Schumacher, Kaltz (c), Briegel [Rummenigge
97], B. Förster, Kh. Förster, Stielike, Magath [Hrubesch 73],
Breitner, Fischer, Dremmler, Littbarski.*
FRANCE *Ettori, Amoros, Bossis, Janvion, Trésor, Giresse, Genghini
[Battiston 50], Lopez 60], Six, Tigana, Platini (c), Rocheteau.*
PENALTY SHOOT-OUT: *Giresse 1-0, Kaltz 1-1, Amoros 2-1,
Breitner 2-2, Rocheteau 3-2, Stielike saved, Six saved, Littbarski
3-3, Platini 4-3, Rummenigge 4-4, Bossis saved, Hrubesch 4-5.*

3rd-place Final

10 July 1982 • José Rico Pérez, Alicante • 28,000 •
Antônio Garrido (POR)

POLAND (2) 3 Szarmach 42, Majewski 45,
Kupcewicz 47
FRANCE (1) 2 Girard 14, Couriol 75

POLAND *Mlynarczyk, Dziuba, Majewski, Janas, Zmuda (c),
Matysik [Wójcicki HT], Lato, Kupcewicz, Szarmach, Boniek, Buncol.*
FRANCE *Castaneda, Amoros, Janvion [Lopez 66], Girard,
Mahut, Trésor (c), Couriol, Tigana [Six 83], Soler, Larios, Bellone.*

Final

11 July 1982 • Bernabéu, Madrid • 90,089 • Arnaldo Coelho (BRZ)

ITALY (0) 3 Rossi 56, Tardelli 68, Altobelli 80
WEST GERMANY (0) 1 Breitner 83

ITALY *Zoff (c), Bergomi, Cabrini, Gentile, Oriali, Collovati, Scirea, Tardelli, Conti, Rossi, Graziani [Altobelli 7, Causio 89].*
W. GERMANY *Schumacher, Kaltz, Briegel, B. Förster, Kh. Förster, Stielike, Littbarski, Dremmler [Hrubesch 62], Breitner, Fischer, Rummenigge (c) [H. Müller 70].*

The first missed penalty in a World Cup Final: Antonio Cabrini shoots wide.

THE HAND OF THE BASKERVILLES

Mexico 1986

TEAMS HAD BECOME fitter since the last World Cup visit to Mexico and appeared to suffer less distress from the altitude – but most of the fancied teams had other problems. The holders Italy came with the same coach and several of the same players but a patchy recent record. France had won all 12 of their matches in 1984, including the European Championship in which Platini scored nine goals in five games. But that was at home, the team had begun to creak a little in the two years since, and there was still no reliable striker.

Maradona was at his peak for Argentina but seemed to lack a quality supporting cast. West Germany had Beckenbauer as manager but no midfield general. Brazil were strong at the back and had Careca up front, but were still relying on their 1982 creative players, who were all over 30: Zico, Sócrates, Falcão, Júnior. Mexico, who'd been doing well under their Yugoslav coach, seemed to have been strengthened by the inclusion of Hugo Sánchez – but had lost 3-0 to England a month earlier and would again have to lean heavily on home support.

England had qualified far more comfortably this time, without losing a match. The messianic Bryan Robson had a troublesome shoulder but there was a quick new striker in Gary Lineker, the First Division's leading scorer. High hopes but fingers crossed. Northern Ireland came through from the same group after holding out for a goalless draw at Wembley and showing their usual grit by winning 1-0 in Romania.

Scotland were there yet again, after a long haul tinged with tragedy. Jock Stein, their manager, had died of a heart attack while watching the 1-1 draw in Cardiff which sent them through to a play-off with Australia. Then the 0-0 draw in Melbourne owed much to Jim Leighton's form in goal. Yet again, the Scots were unfortunate with the draw for the finals, finding themselves in the 'Group of Death' with West Germany, the exciting Danes (in the finals for the first time) and

Uruguay, many people's favourites with their array of world-class defenders and Francescoli in midfield.

FIFA had carried out their threat to increase the number of qualifiers to 24. The second stage mini-leagues were scrapped in favour of a knockout format, a return to the 1970 system but with an extra match. To fit 24 into the 16 needed for the second round, the four third-placed teams with the best records would join the top two in each of six groups.

Above: Brazil's Júnior and Sócrates celebrate the goal against Spain in 1986.

Groups

GROUP A

	P	W	D	L	F	A	PTS
Argentina	3	2	1	0	6	2	5
Italy	3	1	2	0	5	4	4
Bulgaria	3	0	2	1	2	4	2
S. Korea	3	0	1	2	4	7	1

Argentina, Italy and Bulgaria qualified for the second round.

GROUP B

	P	W	D	L	F	A	PTS
Mexico	3	2	1	0	4	2	5
Paraguay	3	1	2	0	4	3	4
Belgium	3	1	1	1	5	5	3
Iraq	3	0	0	3	1	4	0

Mexico, Paraguay and Belgium qualified for the second round.

GROUP C

	P	W	D	L	F	A	PTS
USSR	3	2	1	0	9	1	5
France	3	2	1	0	5	1	5
Hungary	3	1	0	2	2	9	2
Canada	3	0	0	3	0	5	0

USSR and France qualified for the second round.

GROUP D

	P	W	D	L	F	A	PTS
Brazil	3	3	0	0	5	0	6
Spain	3	2	0	1	5	2	4
N. Ireland	3	0	1	2	2	6	1
Algeria	3	0	1	2	1	5	1

Brazil and Spain qualified for the second round.

GROUP E	**P**	**W**	**D**	**L**	**F**	**A**	**PTS**
Denmark	3	3	0	0	9	1	6
W. Germany	3	1	1	1	3	4	3
Uruguay	3	0	2	1	2	7	2
Scotland	3	0	1	2	1	3	1

Denmark, West Germany and Uruguay qualified for the second round.

GROUP F	**P**	**W**	**D**	**L**	**F**	**A**	**PTS**
Morocco	3	1	2	0	3	1	4
England	3	1	1	1	3	1	3
Poland	3	1	1	1	1	3	3
Portugal	3	1	0	2	2	4	2

Morocco, England and Poland qualified for the second round.

2nd Round

15 June 1986 • Azteca, Mexico City • 114,580 • Romualdo Arppi (BRZ)
MEXICO (1) 2 Negrete 34, Servín 61
BULGARIA (0) 0

15 June 1986 • Campo Nuevo, León • 32,277 • Erik Fredriksson (SWE)
BELGIUM (0) (2) 4 Scifo 54, Ceulemans 77, Demol 102, Claesen 108
USSR (1) (2) 3 Belanov 27, 69, pen 111

16 June 1986 • Jalisco, Guadalajara • 45,000 •
Volker Roth (WG)
BRAZIL (1) 4 Sócrates pen 29, Josimar 56,
Edinho 78, Careca pen 83
POLAND (0) 0

16 June 1986 • Cuauhtemoc, Puebla • 26,000 •
Luigi Agnolin (ITA)
ARGENTINA (1) 1 Pasculli 41
URUGUAY (0) 0

17 June 1986 • Olímpico, Mexico City •
71,449 • Carlos Esposito (ARG)
FRANCE (1) 2 Platini 15, Stopyra 57
ITALY (0) 0

17 June 1986 • Universitário, Monterrey • 19,800 •
Zoran Petrovic (YUG)
WEST GERMANY (0) 1 Matthäus 88
MOROCCO (0) 0

18 June 1986 • Azteca, Mexico City • 98,728 •
Jamal Al-Sharif (SYR)
ENGLAND (1) 3 Lineker 31, 72, Beardsley 56
PARAGUAY (0) 0

18 June 1986 • La Corregidora, Queretaro •
38,500 • Jan Keizer (HOL)
SPAIN (1) 5 Butragueño 43, 57, 79, pen 88,
Goikoetxea pen 68
DENMARK (1) 1 J. Olsen pen 32

Quarter-finals

21 June 1986 • Jalisco, Guadalajara • 65,677 •
Ioan Igna (ROM)
FRANCE (1) (1) 1 Platini 41
BRAZIL (1) (1) 1 Careca 17

21 June 1986 • Universitário, Monterrey • 44,386 •
Jesús Díaz Palacio (COL)
WEST GERMANY 0
MEXICO 0 West Germany 4-1 pens.

22 June 1986 • Azteca, Mexico City •
114,580 • Ali Ben Nasser (TUN)
ARGENTINA (0) 2 Maradona 51, 55
ENGLAND (0) 1 Lineker 81

22 June 1986 • Cuauhtemoc, Puebla • 45,000 •
Siegfried Kirschen (EG)
BELGIUM (1) (1) 1 Ceulemans 34
SPAIN (0) (1) 1 Señor 84

Semi-finals

25 June 1986 • Jalisco, Guadalajara • 47,500 •
Luigi Agnolin (ITA)

WEST GERMANY (1) 2 Brehme 9, Völler 89
FRANCE (0) 0

Rudi Völler heads West Germany's equalizer in the 1986 Final.

W. GERMANY *Schumacher, Brehme, Briegel, Eder, Förster, Jakobs, Rummenigge (c) [Völler 57], Matthäus, Allofs, Magath, Rolff.*
FRANCE *Bats, Ayache, Amoros, Fernandez, Bossis, Battiston, Giresse [Vercruysse 71], Tigana, Stopyra, Platini (c), Bellone [Xuereb 66].*

25 June 1986 • Azteca, Mexico City • 110,420 • Antonio Márquez (MEX)

ARGENTINA (0) 2 Maradona 51, 63
BELGIUM (0) 0

ARGENTINA *Pumpido, Cuciuffo, Olarticoechea, Batista, Ruggeri, Brown, Giusti, Enrique, Burruchaga [Bochini 85], Maradona (c), Valdano.*
BELGIUM *Pfaff, Gerets, Renquin [Desmet 53], Vervoort, Demol, Grün, Scifo, Vercauteren, Ceulemans (c), Claesen, Veyt.*

3rd-place Final

28 June 1986 • Cuauhtemoc, Puebla • 21,500 •
George Courtney (ENG)

FRANCE (2) (2) 4 Ferreri 27, Papin 43, Genghini
104, Amoros pen 111
BELGIUM (1) (2) 2 Ceulemans 11, Claesen 73

FRANCE *Rust, Bibard, Amoros, Tigana [Tusseau 84], Le Roux
[Bossis 56], Battiston (c), Vercruysse, Genghini, Papin, Ferreri,
Bellone.*
BELGIUM *Pfaff, Gerets, Renquin [F. Van der Elst HT], Vervoort,
Grün, Demol, Mommens, Scifo [L. Van der Elst 65], Ceulemans
(c), Claesen, Veyt.*

LEADING GOALSCORERS 1986

6	Gary Lineker	ENG	
5	Emilio Butragueño	SPA	1 pen
5	Careca	BRZ	1 pen
5	Diego Maradona	ARG	

*Opposite: Maradona, the
greatest player of his generation,
celebrates Argentina's victory.*

Final

29 June 1986 • Azteca, Mexico City •
114,580 • Romualdo Arppi (BRZ)

ARGENTINA (1) 3 Brown 23, Valdano 56,
Burruchaga 85
WEST GERMANY (0) 2 Rummenigge 74, Völler 82

ARGENTINA *Pumpido, Cuciuffo, Olarticoechea, Enrique,
Ruggeri, Brown, Giusti, Batista, Burruchaga [Trobbiani 89],
Maradona (c), Valdano.*
W. GERMANY *Schumacher, Berthold, Briegel, Jakobs, Förster,
Eder, Matthäus, Brehme, Allofs [Völler HT], Magath [Hoeness
61], Rummenigge (c).*

PENALTIES OF FAME

Italy 1990

NO-ONE WAS unduly surprised when Italy became the first European country to host the World Cup more than once. They'd been the first to host the European Championship twice (before most countries had held it once) and generally knew their way through the corridors of power. That and a strong national team gave them a serious head start. The defence, in which Bergomi was now the captain, had been reinforced by the young Paolo Maldini and another great sweeper in Franco Baresi. But there were problems and controversies up front, where coach Vicini seemed reluctant to use the talents of Roberto Baggio. Much would depend on Vialli, who'd just scored the goals that won Sampdoria the Cup-Winners' Cup.

Lineker equalizes with ten minutes left in the 1990 England v West German semi-final.

Argentina had several of the same players as in 1986, again led by Maradona, but had won only one of their last ten games, 2-1 in Israel. They had to take what comfort they could from their second match being staged on Maradona's home club ground.

West Germany had failed to win the European Championship at home two years earlier but had many more talented players than in 1986. Brehme, Matthäus and Völler were reinforced by world-class newcomers like Buchwald, Kohler and the dashing blond Klinsmann. But Beckenbauer, still the manager, was having to use the veteran Augenthaler as sweeper.

Brazil had a new coach and another strong defence, but no replacements for their old midfield stars. Careca was still there but his obvious partner, the immensely gifted Romário, hadn't played since breaking a leg in March. They were the only team to have beaten Italy this season, and were established as joint second favourites or thereabouts.

Ahead of them in the ratings were the Dutch, back in the finals with a team that lost little in comparison with Cruyff & Co., European Champions arriving with a battery of all-time greats. Rijkaard and Ronald Koeman, the dreadlocked Gullit, van Basten the complete centre-forward; they were the big stumbling block in England's group. Nevertheless England had reason to be cheerful. After their disastrous European finals, Bobby Robson was allowed to stay on and quickly brought in a great new defensive talent in the lightning-quick Des Walker. They qualified without conceding a goal.

The Republic of Ireland, who'd beaten England in Euro '88 and were drawn in the same group again, were coached by Jack Charlton, of 1966 fame, who'd overlooked their midfield skills in favour of an approach that involved banging the ball towards the corner flags to turn opposition defences. It was effective enough to take them to the finals for the first time at the expense of their neighbours from the North.

Scotland, present for the fifth time in a row, again found themselves in the same group as Brazil, but fancied their chances against Sweden, who'd twice drawn 0-0 with England in the qualifiers. And manager Andy Roxburgh wasn't alone in thinking 'we have nothing to fear from Costa Rica'.

Monzón becomes the first player to be sent off in a Final, for a foul on the prostrate Klinsmann.

Groups

GROUP A

	P	W	D	L	F	A	PTS
Italy	3	3	0	0	4	0	6
Czechoslovakia	3	2	0	1	6	3	4
Austria	3	1	0	2	2	3	2
USA	3	0	0	3	2	8	0

Italy and Czechoslovakia qualified for the second round.

GROUP B

	P	W	D	L	F	A	PTS
Cameroon	3	2	0	1	3	5	4
Romania	3	1	1	1	4	3	3
Argentina	3	1	1	1	3	2	3
USSR	3	1	0	2	4	4	2

Cameroon, Romania and Argentina qualified for the second round.

GROUP C

	P	W	D	L	F	A	PTS
Brazil	3	3	0	0	4	1	6
Costa Rica	3	2	0	1	3	2	4
Scotland	3	1	0	2	2	3	2
Sweden	3	0	0	3	3	6	0

Brazil and Costa Rica qualified for the second round.

GROUP D

	P	W	D	L	F	A	PTS
W. Germany	3	2	1	0	10	3	5
Yugoslavia	3	2	0	1	6	5	4
Colombia	3	1	1	1	3	2	3
Emirates	3	0	0	3	2	11	0

West Germany, Yugoslavia and Colombia qualified for the second round.

GROUP E	P	W	D	L	F	A	PTS
Spain	3	2	1	0	5	2	5
Belgium	3	2	0	1	6	3	4
Uruguay	3	1	1	1	2	3	3
S. Korea	3	0	0	3	1	6	0

Spain, Belgium and Uruguay qualified for the second round.

GROUP F	P	W	D	L	F	A	PTS
England	3	1	2	0	2	1	4
Rep. Ireland	3	0	3	0	2	2	3
Holland	3	0	3	0	2	2	3
Egypt	3	0	2	1	1	2	2

England, Republic of Ireland and Holland qualified for the second round. Second and third places decided by drawing of lots.

2nd Round

23 June 1990 • San Paolo, Naples • 50,026 • Tullio Lanese (ITA)
CAMEROON (0) (0) 2 Milla 106, 109
COLOMBIA (0) (0) 1 Redín 116

23 June 1990 • San Nicola, Bari • 15,000 • Siegfried Kirschen (EG)
CZECHOSLOVAKIA (1) 4 Skuhravy 11, 62, 82, Kubík 77
COSTA RICA (0) 1 González 56

24 June 1990 • Delle Alpi Turin • 61,381 • Joël Quiniou (FRA)
ARGENTINA (0) 1 Caniggia 81
BRAZIL (0) 0

24 June 1990 • Giuseppe Meazza, Milan • 74,559 • Juan Carlos Loustau (ARG)
WEST GERMANY (0) 2 Klinsmann 50, Brehme 84
HOLLAND (0) 1 R. Koeman pen 88

25 June 1990 • Luigi Ferraris, Genoa • 31,818 • José Ramiz Wright (BRZ)
REP. IRELAND 0
ROMANIA 0
Ireland 5-4 pens.

25 June 1990 • Olimpico, Rome • 73,303 • George Courtney (ENG)
ITALY (0) 2 Schillaci 65, Serena 83
URUGUAY (0) 0

26 June 1990 • Marc'Antonio Bentegodi, Verona • 34,822 • Aron Schmidhuber (WG)
YUGOSLAVIA (0) (1) 2 Stojkovic 77, 93
SPAIN (0) (1) 1 Salinas 83

26 June 1990 • Renato Dall' Ara, Bologna • 34,520 • Peter Mikkelsen (DEN)
ENGLAND (0) (0) 1 Platt 119
BELGIUM (0) (0) 0

Quarter-finals

30 June 1990 • Comunale, Florence • 38,971 •
Kurt Röthlisberger (SWI)
ARGENTINA 0
YUGOSLAVIA 0
Argentina 3-2 pens.

30 June 1990 • Olimpico, Rome • 73,303 • Carlos
Alberto da Silva Valente (POR)
ITALY (1) 1 Schillaci 38
REP. IRELAND (0) 0

1 July 1990 • Giuseppe Meazza, Milan • 73,347 •
Helmut Kohl (AUT)
WEST GERMANY (1) 1 Matthäus pen 24
CZECHOSLOVAKIA (0) 0

1 July 1990 • San Paolo, Naples • 55,205 •
Edgardo Codesal (MEX)
ENGLAND (1) (2) 3 Platt 25, Lineker pen 83,
pen 104
CAMEROON (0) (2) 2 Kunde pen 61, Ekeke 65

Cameroon, surprise quarter-finalists in only their second World Cup.

Semi-finals

3 July 1990 • San Paolo, Naples • 59,978 • Michel Vautrot (FRA)

ARGENTINA (0) (1) 1 Caniggia 67
ITALY (1) (1) 1 Schillaci 17
Argentina 4-3 pens.

ARGENTINA Goycochea, Serrizuela, Olarticoechea, Simón, Ruggeri, Basualdo [Batista 98], Burruchaga, Giusti, Caniggia, Maradona (c), Calderón [Troglio HT].
ITALY Zenga, Bergomi (c), Maldini, De Agostini, Ferri, Baresi, Donadoni, De Napoli, Schillaci, Giannini [Baggio 75], Vialli [Serena 70].
SENT OFF: Giusti 109.
PENALTY SHOOT-OUT: Baresi 1-0, Serrizuela 1-1, Baggio 2-1, Burruchaga 2-2, De Agostini 3-2, Olarticoechea 3-3, Donadoni saved, Maradona 3-4, Serena saved.

4 July 1990 • Delle Alpi, Turin • 62,628 • José Ramiz Wright (BRZ)

WEST GERMANY (0) (1) 1 Brehme 59
ENGLAND (0) (1) 1 Lineker 80
West Germany 4-3 pens.

W. GERMANY *Illgner, Berthold, Brehme, Matthäus (c), Kohler, Augenthaler, Buchwald, Hässler [Reuter 68], Völler [Riedle 38], Thon, Klinsmann.*
ENGLAND *Shilton, Parker, Pearce, Platt, Butcher (c) [Steven 70], Walker, Wright, Beardsley, Lineker, Gascoigne, Waddle.*
PENALTY SHOOT-OUT: *Lineker 1-0, Brehme 1-1, Beardsley 2-1, Matthäus 2-2, Platt 3-2, Riedle 3-3, Pearce saved, Thon 3-4, Waddle shot over.*

3rd-place Final

7 July 1990 • San Nicola, Bari • 51,426 • Joël Quiniou (FRA)

ITALY (0) 2 Baggio 71, Schillaci pen 85
ENGLAND (0) 1 Platt 81

ITALY *Zenga, Bergomi (c), Maldini, Ancelotti, Vierchowod, Baresi, Ferrara, Giannini [Ferri 90], Schillaci, Baggio, De Agostini [Berti 67].*
ENGLAND *Shilton (c), M. G. Stevens, Dorigo, McMahon [Waddle 72], Walker, Parker, Wright [Webb 72], Steven, Lineker, Platt, Beardsley.*

Toto Schillaci, top scorer in the 1990 tournament.

Final

8 July 1990 • Olimpico, Rome • 73,603 • Edgardo Codesal (MEX)

WEST GERMANY (0) 1 Brehme pen 84
ARGENTINA (0) 0

W. GERMANY *Illgner, Berthold [Reuter 73], Brehme, Buchwald, Kohler, Augenthaler, Hässler, Matthäus (c), Littbarski, Völler, Klinsmann.*
ARGENTINA *Goycochea, Simón, Sensini, Basualdo, Serrizuela, Ruggeri [Monzón HT], Burruchaga [Calderón 53], Troglio, Lorenzo, Maradona (c), Dezotti.*
SENT OFF: *Monzón 64, Dezotti 86.*

LEADING GOALSCORERS 1990

6	Salvatore Schillaci	ITA	1 pen
5	Tomás Skuhravy	CZE	
4	Michel	SPA	1 pen
4	Roger Milla	CAM	
4	Lothar Matthäus	WG	1 pen
4	Gary Lineker	ENG	2 pen

THE LONG DROUGHT

USA 1994

IF FIFA HOPED that awarding the World Cup to the land of the dollar would at last crack the supposedly lucrative United States market, it was a triumph of hope over experience. But at least the infrastructure wasn't bad. What visitors were likely to see were matches played in well-appointed stadia, with excellent transport facilities, catering services and communications, an experienced and minimal police presence, and the highest average crowds in World Cup history. If the price was allowing a mediocre USA team free entry, it was worth every cent.

Of the stronger countries, a reunified Germany had a new coach but rather too many old players, though Klinsmann was in his pomp and Sammer a powerful recruit from East Germany. Brazil were without four regular central defenders but others simply stepped off the conveyor belt, and Romário had just scored 30 goals in 33 league games for Barcelona as well as the two goals that sent Brazil through at Uruguay's expense. Italy, who'd rather staggered over the finishing line, were still strong at the back but again in search of a reliable goalscorer.

Argentina had gone 31 matches without losing, which included winning the Copa América twice in a row, but a 5-0 home defeat by Colombia made them recall the 33-year-old Maradona to help them squeeze through in a play-off, beating Australia with a deflected goal.

Colombia, still led by Valderrama, with Asprilla a new threat in attack, were naturally included among the favourites. So too, for the first time, were a team from Africa. Nigeria had just won the African Nations Cup with a blend of skill and power that people had been expecting from the continent for years. Yekini, Okacha, Amunike and Amokachi were expected to become big names in the forthcoming month.

For the first time since they entered the World Cup, none of the four British countries reached the finals, but the Republic of Ireland were there again, still playing the same way under Jack Charlton but qualifying on goal difference and unlikely to figure at the sharp end of the tournament, especially as it was being played in fearful heat and humidity (FIFA again scheduled some noontime kick-offs). Nigeria, we were allowed to suppose, would be rather less apprehensive.

Brazil's Romário, their top goalscorer.

Groups

GROUP A

	P	W	D	L	F	A	PTS
Romania	3	2	0	1	5	5	6
Switzerland	3	1	1	1	5	4	4
USA	3	1	1	1	3	3	4
Colombia	3	1	0	2	4	5	3

Romania, Switzerland and USA qualified for the second round.

GROUP B

	P	W	D	L	F	A	PTS
Brazil	3	2	1	0	6	1	7
Sweden	3	1	2	0	6	4	5
Russia	3	1	0	2	7	6	3
Cameroon	3	0	1	2	3	11	1

Brazil and Sweden qualified for the second round.

GROUP C

	P	W	D	L	F	A	PTS
Germany	3	2	1	0	5	3	7
Spain	3	1	2	0	6	4	5
S. Korea	3	0	2	1	4	5	2
Bolivia	3	0	1	2	1	4	1

Germany and Spain qualified for the second round.

GROUP D

	P	W	D	L	F	A	PTS
Nigeria	3	2	0	1	6	2	6
Bulgaria	3	2	0	1	6	3	6
Argentina	3	2	0	1	6	3	6
Greece	3	0	0	3	0	10	0

Nigeria, Bulgaria and Argentina qualified for the second round.

GROUP E	**P**	**W**	**D**	**L**	**F**	**A**	**PTS**
Mexico	3	1	1	1	3	3	4
Rep. Ireland	3	1	1	1	2	2	4
Italy	3	1	1	1	2	2	4
Norway	3	1	1	1	1	1	4

Mexico, Republic of Ireland and Italy qualified for the second round. Ireland placed second as a result of beating Italy. The only time all four teams finished with the same number of points.

GROUP F	**P**	**W**	**D**	**L**	**F**	**A**	**PTS**
Holland	3	2	0	1	4	3	6
Saudi Arabia	3	2	0	1	4	3	6
Belgium	3	2	0	1	2	1	6
Morocco	3	0	0	3	2	5	0

Holland, Saudi Arabia and Belgium qualified for the second round.

2nd Round

2 July 1994 • Soldier Field, Chicago • 60,246 •
Kurt Röthlisberger (SWI)
GERMANY (3) 3 Völler 6, 40, Klinsmann 11,
BELGIUM (1) 2 Grün 8, Albert 89

2 July 1994 • Robert F. Kennedy, Washington DC •
53,121 • Mario van der Ende (HOL)
SPAIN (1) 3 Hierro 15, Luis Enrique 74,
Beguiristain pen 87
SWITZERLAND (0) 0

3 July 1994 • Cotton Bowl, Dallas • 60,277 •
Renato Marsiglia (BRZ)
SWEDEN (1) 3 Dahlin 6, K.Andersson 51, 88
SAUDI ARABIA (0) 1 Al-Ghesheyan 85

3 July 1994 • Rose Bowl, Pasadena • 90,469 •
Pierluigi Pairetto (ITA)
ROMANIA (2) 3 Dumitrescu 11, 18, Hagi 56
ARGENTINA (1) 2 Batistuta pen 16, Balbo 75

4 July 1994 • Citrus Bowl, Orlando • 61,355 •
Peter Mikkelsen (DEN)
HOLLAND (2) 2 Bergkamp 11, Jonk 41
REP. IRELAND (0) 0

_Opposite: Big Jack engages in a little
touchline debate during Ireland's group
match with Mexico._

4 July 1994 • Stanford, Palo Alto • 84,147 • Joël
Quiniou (FRA)
BRAZIL (0) 1 Bebeto 74
USA (0) 0

5 July 1994 • Foxboro, Boston • 54,367 • Arturo
Brizio Carter (MEX)
ITALY (0) (1) 2 R. Baggio 88, pen 102
NIGERIA (1) (1) 1 Amunike 26

5 July 1994 • Giants Stadium, New Jersey •
71,030 • Jamal Al-Sharif (SYR)
BULGARIA (1) (1) 1 Stoitchkov 7
MEXICO (1) (1) 1 García Aspe pen 18,

Quarter-finals

9 July 1994 • Foxboro, Boston • 54,605 • Sándor Puhl (HUN)
ITALY (1) 2 D. Baggio 26, R. Baggio 88
SPAIN (0) 1 Caminero 59

9 July 1994 • Cotton Bowl, Dallas • 63,998 • Rodrigo Badilla (COS)
BRAZIL (0) 3 Romário 52, Bebeto 62, Branco 81
HOLLAND (0) 2 Bergkamp 64, Winter 76

10 July 1994 • Giants Stadium, New Jersey • 72,416 • José Torres Cadena (COL)
BULGARIA (0) 2 Stoitchkov 75, Letchkov 78
GERMANY (0) 1 Matthäus pen 48

10 July 1994 • Stanford, Palo Alto • 81,715 • Philip Don (ENG)
SWEDEN (0) (1) 2 Brolin 79, K. Andersson 115
ROMANIA (0) (1) 2 Raducioiu 88, 101

Opposite: The bristling Stoitchkov celebrates his goal against Mexico in the second round.

Semi-finals

13 July 1994 • Giants Stadium, New Jersey •
77,094 • Joël Quiniou (FRA)

ITALY (2) 2 R. Baggio 20, 25
BULGARIA (1) 1 Stoitchkov pen 44

ITALY *Pagliuca, Mussi, Benarrivo, Berti, Costacurta, Maldini (c),
Donadoni, Albertini, D. Baggio [Conte 55], R. Baggio [Signori
70], Casiraghi.*
BULGARIA *Mikhailov (c), Kiriakov, Hubchev, Ivanov, Tsvetanov,
Letchkov, Yankov, Sirakov, Balakov, Stoitchkov [Genchev 78],
Kostadinov [Yordanov 71].*

13 July 1994 • Rose Bowl, Pasadena • 84,569 •
José Torres Cadena (COL)

BRAZIL (0) 1 Romário 80
SWEDEN (0) 0

BRAZIL *Taffarel, Jorginho, Branco, Mauro Silva, Aldair,
Márcio Santos, Mazinho [Raí HT], Dunga (c), Bebeto, Romário,
Zinho.*
SWEDEN *Ravelli, R. Nilsson, Ljung, Mild, P. Andersson,
Björklund, Brolin, Thern (c), K. Andersson, Ingesson, Dahlin
[Rehn 68].*
SENT OFF: *Thern 63.*

*Opposite: The moment Brazil
win the World Cup for a
record fourth time.*

3rd-place Final

16 July 1994 • Rose Bowl, Pasadena • 83,716 •
Ali Mohammed Bujsaim (UAE)

SWEDEN (4) 4 Brolin 8, Mild 30, Larsson 37, K.
Andersson 39
BULGARIA (0) 0

SWEDEN *Ravelli, R. Nilsson (c), Kåmark, Schwarz,
P. Andersson, Björklund, Mild, Brolin, K. Andersson, Ingesson,
Larsson [Limpar 78].*
BULGARIA *Mikhailov (c) [Nikolov HT], Kiriakov, Hubchev,
Ivanov [Kremenliev 41], Tsvetanov, Lechkov, Yankov, Sirakov
[Yordanov HT], Balakov, Stoitchkov, Kostadinov.*

Final

17 July 1994 • Rose Bowl, Pasadena • 94,194 •
Sándor Puhl (HUN)

BRAZIL 0
ITALY 0
Brazil 3-2 pens.

BRAZIL *Taffarel, Jorginho [Cafú 21], Branco, Mazinho, Aldair, Márcio Santos, Mauro Silva, Dunga (c), Romário, Bebeto, Zinho [Viola 105].*
ITALY *Pagliuca, Mussi [Apolloni 34], Benarrivo, Berti, Maldini, Baresi (c), Donadoni, Albertini, Massaro, R. Baggio, D. Baggio [Evani 94].*
PENALTY SHOOT-OUT: *Baresi shot over, Márcio Santos saved, Albertini 1-0, Romário 1-1, Evani 2-1, Branco 2-2, Massaro saved, Dunga 2-3, R. Baggio shot over.*

LEADING GOALSCORERS 1994

6	Oleg Salenko	RUS	1 pen
6	Hristo Stoitchkov	BUL	3 pen
5	Jürgen Klinsmann	GER	
5	Roberto Baggio	ITA	1 pen
5	Romário	BRZ	
5	Kennet Andersson	SWE	

The leading scorers in the last five tournaments have scored six goals.

*Opposite: Abel Lafleur's
famous World Cup trophy.*

WORLD CUP RECORDS

MOST NEW CAPS IN A GAME

10	Brazil	1930	v Yugoslavia
10	Argentina	1934	v Sweden
9	Dutch East Indies	1938	v Hungary
8	Brazil	1934	v Spain

YOUNGEST REFEREES

yrs	days			
27	62	Francisco Matteucci	URU	1930
28	224	Ivan Eklind	SWE	1934
30	40	Peter Mikkelsen	DEN	1990
30	153	Louis Baert	BEL	1934
30	231	José María Codesal	URU	1958
30	262	Ramón Barreto	URU	1970

Eklind was also the youngest in a Final: 28 yrs 238 days.

SMALLEST CROWDS

300	1930	Romania	v	Peru	Montevideo
2,000	1954	Turkey	v	S. Korea	Geneva
2,823	1958	Wales	v	Hungary	Stockholm
3,580	1950	Switzerland	v	Mexico	Pôrto Alegre
3,993	1938	Cuba	v	Romania	Toulouse
4,444	1930	France	v	Mexico	Montevideo

Lowest for a Final

45,124	1938	Italy	v	Hungary	Paris

OLDEST TO SCORE A HAT-TRICK

yrs	days			
29	329	Pedro Cea	URU	1930
29	95	Teófilo Cubillas	PER	1978
28	270	Preben Elkjaer	DEN	1986

Cubillas 2 penalties.

PLAYED FOR TWO COUNTRIES

Luis Monti	1930 ARG	1934 ITA
Atilio Demaría	1930 ARG	1934 ITA
José Santamaría	1954 URU	1962 SPA
Ferenc Puskás	1954 HUN	1962 SPA
José Altafini	1958 BRZ	1962 ITA

Altafini was known as 'Mazzola' in Brazil.

MOST SENDINGS-OFF IN A MATCH

3	1938	Brazil v Czechoslovakia
3	1954	Brazil v Hungary

BIGGEST CROWDS

205,000	1950	BRZ	v URU	Rio de Janeiro
152,772	1950	BRZ	v SPA	Rio de Janeiro
142,429	1950	BRZ	v YUG	Rio de Janeiro
138,886	1950	BRZ	v SWE	Rio de Janeiro
114,600	1986	MEX	v PAR	Mexico City
114,580	1986	MEX	v BUL	Mexico City
114,580	1986	ARG	v ENG	Mexico City
114,580	1986	ARG	v WG	Mexico City

OLDEST REFEREES

yrs	days			
53	236	George Reader	ENG	1950
51	284	Mario Vianna	BRZ	1954
50	140	Alfred Birlem	GER	1938
50	72	Jack Mowat	SCO	1958
50	34	Antonio Márquez	MEX	1986
50	03	Leo Lemesic	YUG	1958

Reader had been taken off the Football League list for being too old.

MOST GOALS IN A TOURNAMENT

27	Hungary	1954
25	W. Germany	1954
23	France	1958

WON TOURNAMENT AFTER LOSING A MATCH

1954	West Germany
1974	West Germany
1978	Argentina

WINNING MARGINS

9	Hungary	1954	v S. Korea	9-0
9	Yugoslavia	1974	v Zaire	9-0
9	Hungary	1982	v El Salvador	10-1
8	Sweden	1938	v Cuba	8-0
8	Uruguay	1950	v Bolivia	8-0

YOUNGEST CAPTAINS

22	33	Turgay Seren	TUR	1954
22	193	Ladislav Novák	CZE	1954
22	222	Harry Keough	USA	1950

HAT-TRICKS

2	Sándor Kocsis	HUN	1954
2	Just Fontaine	FRA	1958
2	Gerd Müller	WG	1970

MOST GOALS IN A GAME

12	1954	Austria	7	Switzerland	5
11	1938	Brazil	6	Poland	5
11	1954	Hungary	8	W. Germany	3
11	1982	Hungary	10	El Salvador	1
10	1958	France	7	Paraguay	3

MATCHES WON FROM 3 GOALS DOWN

1954	Austria	v Switzerland	7-5
1966	Portugal	v N. Korea	5-3

YOUNGEST PLAYERS IN A FINAL

yrs	days			
17	249	Pelé	BRZ	1958
18	201	Giuseppe Bergomi	ITA	1982
19	344	Rubén Morán	URU	1950

CONSECUTIVE DRAWS

4	Ireland	1990
3	Wales	1958
3	England	1958
3	Cameroon	1982
3	Holland	1990

CAPTAIN IN MOST TOURNAMENTS

3	Billy Wright	ENG	1950–54–58
3	Ladislav Novák	CZE	1954–58–62
3	Björn Nordqvist	SWE	1970–74–78
3	Diego Maradona	ARG	1986–90–94

YOUNGEST GOALSCORERS

yrs	days			
17	239	Pelé	BRZ	1958
18	93	Manuel Rosas	MEX	1930
18	197	Nicolae Kovács	ROM	1930

YOUNGEST TO SCORE A HAT-TRICK

yrs	days			
17	244	Pelé	BRZ	1958
19	197	Edmund Conen	GER	1934
20	255	Bert Patenaude	BRZ	1930
20	261	Flórián Albert	HUN	1962

MOST GOALS IN A TOURNAMENT

13	Just Fontaine	FRA	1958	
11	Sándor Kocsis	HUN	1954	
10	Gerd Müller	WG	1970	1 pen.
9	Eusébio	POR	1966	4 pen.
8	Guillermo Stábile	ARG	1930	
8	Ademir	BRZ	1950	

SCORED IN MOST CONSECUTIVE MATCHES

6	Just Fontaine	FRA	1958
6	Jairzinho	BRZ	1970
5	Gerd Müller	WG	1970

SCORED IN MORE THAN ONE FINAL

2	Vavá	BRZ	1958 & 1962
2	Pelé	BRZ	1958 & 1970
2	Paul Breitner	WG	1974 & 1982

MOST GOALS IN FINALS

3	Vavá	BRZ	1958 & 1962
3	Geoff Hurst	ENG	1966
3	Pelé	BRZ	1958 & 1970

MOST TOURNAMENTS AS COACH

4	Sepp Herberger	WG	1938–54–58–62
4	Walter Winterbottom	ENG	1950–54–58–62
4	Helmut Schön	WG	1966–70–74–78
4	Lajos Baróti	HUN	1958–62–66–78

Appointed for France '98

4	Carlos Alberto Parreira	BRZ	1982–90–94–98
4	Bora Milutinovic	YUG	1986–90–94–98

FASTEST GOALS

secs

15	Václav Masek	CZE	1962	v MEX
24	Ernst Lehner	GER	1934	v AUT
27	Bryan Robson	ENG	1982	v FRA
35	Émile Veinante	FRA	1938	v BEL
35	Arne Nyberg	SWE	1938	v HUN
37	Bernard Lacombe	FRA	1978	v ITA

PLAYED IN MOST TOURNAMENTS

5	Antonio Carbajal	MEX	1950–54–58–62–66
4	Pelé	BRZ	1958–62–66–70
4	Karl-Heinz Schnellinger	WG	1958–62–66–70
4	Uwe Seeler	WG	1958–62–66–70
4	Gianni Rivera	ITA	1962–66–70–74
4	Pedro Rocha	URU	1962–66–70–74
4	Wladyslaw Zmuda	POL	1974–78–82–86
4	Lothar Matthäus	WG/GER	1982–86–90–94
4	Diego Maradona	ARG	1982–86–90–94

LONGEST PLAYING SPANS

yrs	days			
16	25	Antonio Carbajal	MEX	1950–66
16	17	Hugo Sánchez	MEX	1978–94
15	346	Elias Figueroa	CHI	1966–82

CONSECUTIVE MATCHES UNBEATEN

13	Brazil	1958–66
11	Uruguay	1930–54
11	Brazil	1970–74
11	Brazil	1978–82
11	WG/Germany	1990–94
10	Italy	1982–86

WORLD CUP WINNER AS PLAYER AND COACH

Mário Zagallo	BRZ	1958–62	1970
Franz Beckenbauer	WG	1974	1990

Beckenbauer was also a losing finalist as a player (1966) and coach (1986).

SCORED IN MOST TOURNAMENTS

4	Uwe Seeler	WG	1958–62–66–70
4	Pelé	BRZ	1958–62–66–70
3	Joe Jordan	SCO	1974–78–82
3	Grzegorz Lato	POL	1974–78–82
3	Andrzej Szarmach	POL	1974–78–82
3	Dominique Rocheteau	FRA	1978–82–86
3	Michel Platini	FRA	1978–82–86
3	Julio Salinas	SPA	1986–90–94
3	Diego Maradona	ARG	1982–86–94
3	Rüdi Völler	WG/GER	1986–90–94
3	Lothar Matthäus	WG/GER	1986–90–94

MOST GOALS BY ONE TEAM

10-1	Hungary	1982	v El Salvador
9-0	Hungary	1954	v S. Korea
9-0	Yugoslavia	1974	v Zaire

MOST MATCHES

21	Uwe Seeler	WG	1958–70
21	Wladyslaw Zmuda	POL	1974–86
21	Diego Maradona	ARG	1982–94
21	Lothar Matthäus	WG/GER	1982–94
20	Grzegorz Lato	POL	1974–82
19	Wolfgang Overath	WG	1966–74
19	Berti Vogts	WG	1970–78
19	Karl-Heinz Rummenigge	WG	1978–86

British

17	Peter Shilton	ENG	1982–90

MOST GOALS IN TOTAL

14	Gerd Müller	WG	1970–74	1 pen.
13	Just Fontaine	FRA	1958	
12	Pelé	BRZ	1958–70	
11	Sándor Kocsis	HUN	1954	
10	Helmut Rahn	WG	1954–58	
10	Teófilo Cubillas	PER	1970–78	2 pen.
10	Grzegorz Lato	POL	1974–82	
10	Gary Lineker	ENG	1986–90	2 pen.

Best of other British

5	Peter McParland	NIR	1958
4	Joe Jordan	SCO	1974–82
2	Ivor Allchurch	WAL	1958

Four players have scored one goal each for the Republic of Ireland: Kevin Sheedy, Niall Quinn (1990), Ray Houghton, John Aldridge (1994).

OLDEST PLAYER IN A FINAL

yrs	days			
40	133	Dino Zoff	ITA	1982
37	241	Gunnar Gren	SWE	1958
37	212	Jan Jongbloed	HOL	1978
37	32	Nilton Santos	BRZ	1962

rs   days

YOUNGEST PLAYERS

7	41	Norman Whiteside	NIR	1982
7	235	Pelé	BRZ	1958
7	353	Rigobert Song	CAM	1994

Edu, aged 16, was in Brazil's 1966 squad.

SHORTEST FINALS CAREERS

ins

Marcelo Trobbiani	ARG	1986	v WG
Khemais Labidi	TUN	1978	v MEX
Miguel Pardeza	SPA	1990	v BEL
Magnus Erlingmark	SWE	1994	v RUS
Petar Mikhtarski	BUL	1994	v MEX
Corneliu Papura	ROM	1994	v COL & ARG
Ion Vladoiu	ROM	1994	v SWI
Miguel Angel Oviedo	ARG	1978	v PER
Marco Etcheverry	BOL	1994	v GER

British

Kerry Dixon	ENG	1986	v POL

BOOKINGS IN A MATCH

	1990	Austria (5)	v	USA (4)	1990
	1994	Italy (5)	v	Nigeria (4)	1994
	1986	Mexico (5)	v	W. Germany (3)	1986
	1994	Bulgaria (4)	v	Greece (4)	1994
	1994	Spain (4)	v	Switzerland (4)	1994
	1994	Germany (5)	v	Bulgaria (3)	1994

*A tenth player (another Austrian) was sent off in the 1990 match.
Two players were sent off in the Mexico-WG match, one of whom
had previously been booked. Italy also had another player sent off.*

CLEAN SHEETS

10	Peter Shilton	ENG	1982–90
8	Sepp Maier	WG	1974–78
8	Emerson Leão	BRZ	1974–78
7	Gylmar	BRZ	1958–66
6	Gordon Banks	ENG	1966–70

CONSECUTIVE CLEAN SHEETS

5	Walter Zenga	ITA	1990
4	Gylmar	BRZ	1958
4	Gordon Banks	ENG	1966
4	Emerson Leão	BRZ	1974
4	Sepp Maier	WG	1978
4	Emerson Leão	BRZ	1978
4	Peter Shilton	ENG	1982
4	Carlos	BRZ	1986

MINUTES WITHOUT CONCEDING A GOAL

517	Walter Zenga	ITA	1990
500	Peter Shilton	ENG	1982–86
475	Sepp Maier	WG	1974–78
458	Emerson Leão	BRZ	1978
442	Gordon Banks	ENG	1966
401	Carlos	BRZ	1986

OLDEST CAPTAINS

yrs days

40	292	Peter Shilton	ENG	1990
40	133	Dino Zoff	ITA	1982
37	343	Manuel Bento	POR	1986

Outfield players

36	308	Morten Olsen	DEN	1986

GOALS IN A GAME

5	Oleg Salenko	RUS	1994	v CAM	1 pen.
4	Ernest Wilimowski	POL	1938	v BRZ	
4	Ademir	BRZ	1950	v SWE	
4	Sándor Kocsis	HUN	1954	v WG	
4	Just Fontaine	FRA	1958	v WG	
4	Eusébio	POR	1966	v NKO	2 pen.
4	Emilio Butragueño	SPA	1986	v DEN	1 pen.

Leônidas (BRZ) and Gustav Wetterström (SWE), who scored three against Poland and Cuba respectively in 1938, were once credited with four, as was Juan Schiaffino (URU), who scored twice against Bolivia in 1950.

OLDEST PLAYERS

rs	days			
2	39	Roger Milla	CAM	1994
1	00	Pat Jennings	NIR	1986
0	292	Peter Shilton	ENG	1990
0	133	Dino Zoff	ITA	1982
9	260	Angel Labruna	ARG	1958
9	259	Joseph-Antoine Bell	CAM	1994
9	145	Stanley Matthews	ENG	1954
8	246	Vítor Damas	POR	1986

A member of the Cameroon delegation claimed Milla was 46!

OLDEST GOALSCORERS

rs	days			
2	39	Roger Milla	CAM	1994
7	236	Gunnar Gren	SWE	1958
6	279	Obdulio Varela	URU	1954
6	64	Tom Finney	ENG	1958
5	279	John Aldridge	EIR	1994
5	264	Nils Liedholm	SWE	1958
5	67	Safet Susic	YUG	1990

Milla also scored in two matches in 1990 aged 38.

CONSECUTIVE MATCHES WITHOUT A WIN

7	Bulgaria	1962–94
3	Mexico	1930–62
1	Uruguay	1970–90
1	South Korea	1954–94

South Korea, who've reached the 1998 finals, have yet to win a match.

MATCHES AS CAPTAIN

6	Diego Maradona	ARG	1986–94
4	Dino Zoff	ITA	1978–82
3	Kaziu Deyna	POL	1974–78

REFEREES: MOST SENDINGS-OFF

5	Joël Quiniou	FRA	1986–94
4	Jamal Al-Sharif	SYR	1986–94
3	Paul von Hertzka	HUN	1938
3	Arthur Ellis	ENG	1954
3	Jesús Díaz Palacio	COL	1986
3	Michel Vautrot	FRA	1990
3	Arturo Brizio Carter	MEX	1994s

Von Hertzka and Ellis in a single match.

REFEREED MOST MATCHES

8	Joël Quiniou	FRA	1986–94
7	John Langenus	BEL	1930–38
7	Mervyn Griffiths	WAL	1950–58
7	Juan Gardeazábal	SPA	1958–66

PICTURE CREDITS

Actionimages: 103, 108, 117. **Allsport:** Hulton Getty 7, Hulton Getty 23, 57, David Leah 95, Ben Radford 112. **Beejay Soccer Enterprises:** 19, 27, 35, 36, 50. **Hulton Getty:** 17, 25. **Colorsport:** John Varley 61, 65, John Varley 70, 78, 96, 98, 105. **Empics:** Neal Simpson 115. **MSI:** 55, 63, 76. **Popperfoto:** 5, 9, 10, 12, 38, 42, 44, 48, 86, 88, 93, 110.